PREFACE

It was not easy to select a suitable title for this work in which we sought to achieve two main objectives.

One aim has been to describe in considerable detail a course of soft tissue manipulative treatments: not merely describing the technique itself in general terms, but taking each treatment session in logical sequence and describing every item of manipulation. The line drawings, showing muscle origins and insertions, muscle groupings and various structural relationships are as full as our limited artistic skill has been able to make them. We have found from experience that, for example, a drawing of muscles of the left arm is sometimes difficult to follow when working on the right arm.

In so many text books on anatomy it is customary to give a front view of the body with a dividing line down the middle showing, on one side of this line, the superficial muscles and, on the other side of the line, a deep layer. Diagrams of this kind are not always easy to follow. We have tried to overcome such difficulties by including drawings or diagrams of both sides at each level. Although this will undoubtedly make identification much simpler it must not be treated as an excuse for not knowing one's anatomy very thoroughly. This means not only muscle anatomy but also acupuncture meridian and point anatomy.

To the extent that the treatments, and details of each, form a logical and necessary sequence the Treatment can appropriately be said to be 'Progressive'.

The term 'Vitality' also seems suitable inasmuch as there is a progressive release of life-sustaining energy for optimum functioning. 'Vitality' or 'Energy' is here used in a very wide sense to include all vital fluids, blood and lymph as well as the 'energy' known to acupuncturists as Ki or Ch'i, which flows through the Meridians and all connecting channels.

No two-word title, nor sentence even, is able to describe our other main aim. As soon as one tries to explain that this soft-tissue manipulative treatment is *not* a therapy, that is to say it is not designed to 'cure' nor to alleviate disease symptoms but is 'preventive', the question is flung at one: "To prevent what?". The answer, 'to prevent disease', is not enough — for we look upon our method as 'evolutionary'. In its turn this requires even more explanation and justification. We will try to make it clear in the course of the book what the treatment is about, how it works, and give reasons for it being done.

The discerning reader will be able to detect enough of our medicine-philosophical background and spiritual orientation to appreciate the worth-whileness of a technique that helps man to walk upright (Ecc.VII, 29.).

Inevitably there will be a few practitioners to whom the spiritual significance of their work means little or nothing. They want to get on with the physical treatment without having first to consider what to them appears quite irrelevant. To those few the technique will not be fully workable because of their own attitude of mind. It is our sincere belief that there is a growing number of therapists hungry for understandable deep reasons for doing what they do; practitioners who more and more are realizing that 'healing' is not just a covering up or temporarily getting rid of a few ugly or distressing symptoms. 'Healing' means 'making whole once again as it should be'.

In this book we are definitely *not* going to expound any religious or spiritual doctrines: not only is it unnecessary, it would indeed be out of place to do so, because the *physical manipulations* described herein must be operable by any practioner of any religion or none on a client of any religion or none.

We are satisfied that any human being whose physical dynamic posture is *habitually* upright will, by that very virtue, be led into the way of truth *proper to him in his circumstances,* and it is not for a practitioner to decide that.

The upright will be healthy, and not be prey to diseases. Health is a living state of dynamic balancings between *all* the factors that make up the whole man. How a person habitually sits, stands, moves or walks about, reveals that person's attitude to Life. If it is integrated and upright on one level it will tend to be so on all levels.

If it were to be done as fully as we could wish, it would require a volume on its own to acknowledge all the sources which contribute to the development of our Progressive Vitality method and technique. We shall of necessity therefore, have to limit our acknowledgements to special mention of a few names, and in a general way express our gratitude to the many whose names are not here included.

To a deep friendship and long association with Doctor Dorothy Mazel we owe a great deal, and for her teaching and encouragement which led us to delve into little-known fields.

Even though our personal contact with Doctor Marjorie Swanson was limited to a course of lectures delivered by her at the Institute of General Semantics' seminar held at Bard College, Poughkeepsie, Conn., U.S.A., which we attended in 1956, the information she gave us on colloidal structure and behaviour resulted in a valuable turning point in one of our lines of thinking.

On the question, What constitutes correct posture for human beings?, we are indebted (in addition to such works as Diagnosis & Treatment of Postural Defects by Dr. Winthrop Morgan Phelps, and various standard text books on Osteopathy and Cheiropractic) to Doctor Wilfred Barlow, with whom we had enlightening conversations; and to Doctor Ida P. Rolf, with whom we had an intensive five week course of instruction in her 'processing' method. Although we were ourselves processed by Doctor Rolf, and benefitted considerably thereby, her processing technique was unsuitable for our purposes. Nevertheless the order in which Doctor Rolf dealt with muscle structures and groups appeared logical; thus we have kept, with only such modifications as we felt were needed by an 'acupuncture meridian orienta-tion', the sequence she taught us in 1957.

Our principal text-book study of relaxation has been Progressive Relaxation by Dr. Edmund Jacobson (University of Chicago Press), but, of course, we have gleaned much of great value from other writers on relaxation, and from personally trying out the different methods, including having a practical course of Yoga.

To all these and to the many not listed but who have helped us so much we offer our sincere and grateful thanks.

INTRODUCTION

According to several cultural traditions, in widely different parts of the globe, there was a time when man lived in a higher, purer, and nobler way than that in which he now lives. The reason for his present unhappy state being his disregard for, or disobedience to, certain Laws of Nature.

In the Far Eastern tradition of the Nei Ching[1] we learn:

The Yellow Emperor once addressed T'ien Shih the divinely inspired teacher: "I have heard that in ancient times the people lived to be over a hundred years, and yet they remained active and did not become decrepit in their activities. But nowadays people reach only half of that age and yet become decrepit and failing. Is it because the world changes from generation to generation? or is it that mankind is becoming negligent of the laws of nature?"

'Chi Po answered: "In ancient times those people who understood the way of self-cultivation patterned themselves upon the two principles in nature and they lived in harmony with the great rules of the protection of life . . ."

In the Near Eastern tradition of the Old Testament we are also taught that Man has fallen[3]. His life-span after the Fall, but before the Flood, was 120 years[4] but is now a mere 70[5].

If we apply to Man the formula for a proper life-span that applies to other classes and species, we find the calculation works out to the hundred and twenty. It being worked out on the basis that a life-span is equal to five times the length of time taken to reach maturity. Man is not fully mature until the last wisdom tooth has come through; this happens between the ages of twenty and twenty-four. Thus, according to the general Macrobiotic principle, man's life-span should be between one hundred and one hundred and twenty.

According to some other traditions, again in quite different parts of the world, Man has not fallen but is still in the process of evolving and has not yet reached what he is ultimately destined to become. This is exemplified in the Tibetan Chi-Schara-Badgan lamaistic teaching.[6] In the West we have, of course, the evolutionary theories, such as those of Charles Darwin.

[1] Huang Ti Nei Ching Su Wen translated by Ilza Veith, M.A., Ph.D.' (Baltimore, The Williams & Wilkins Company, 1949).
[2] The principles of Unification and Diversification, Yang and Yin.
[3] Gen. 3, 6-7.
[4] Gen. 6, 4. My Spirit shall certainly not remain among these men for ever, because they are flesh, but their days shall be an hundred and twenty years. (Septuagint).
[5] Ps. 89 (90). As for the days of our years, in them are seventy years; and if men should be in strength, eighty years: and what is more than these would be labour and trouble; for weakness overtakes us, and we shall be chastened. (Septuagint).
[6] Tibetische Medezin-Philosophie, P. Cyrill von Korvin-Krazinski, Origo Verlag.

Almost wherever we look we find a recognition that present-day man is not what he could or should be[1] : and this recognition does not require anyone to take sides on the question of 'Fall or Evolution?'

We have, in the West, the combined pattern that Man evolved or was developed (made from clay) *and* fell. From this point of view his reaching the proper goal has been delayed by the Fall. From the Orthodox Christian viewpoint this is the reason for there being a Second or New Adam through whom the destiny of Man will be reached.

Whether we accept or reject the idea that in the legendary past Man was happier and healthier than he is now matters very little provided that there is the recognition and acceptance of the fact that Man *could and should* be different, i.e. *better* than he now is.

As soon as we acknowledge that Man is nowhere near the peak of perfection, or highest possible for him, we begin seriously to think about what he could or should become; then we look for ways and means of reaching out towards a higher status, functioning and purpose. In fact we ask, What is normal?

Throughout this work whenever we use the expression 'normal' we mean 'according to the norm or standard of what is appropriate'. In other words, we do *not* mean 'average'. A person in average health is far far below the standard of what health should be.

In an attempt to establish and define a standard of 'what it should be', we must start our thinking with basic assumptions of some sort; and work on from there, always prepared, however, to change our premises if we should find our conclusions seem unsatisfactory.

Basic Assumptions:

Relatedness. Absolute isolation or absolute independence is not possible: everything in this world is, in some way, related to everything else. Ordinarily, however, we do not need to take into account more than a few relationships .

Functioning. Man, in common with all living creatures, is an organism-as-a-whole-functioning-in-environments.

We use the term 'functioning' to make it quite clear that our idea of Man is not the idea of something with a static structure. Man has dynamic pattern. The organism, the whole organism, lives, moves, changes, in environments that are also living, moving, changing. Thus when we talk of 'structure' we mean dynamic structure.

Levels. We assume, too, that there are different levels of structure or patterning. for convenience we consider, in our context, significant levels to be distinguishable into three; and our expression 'functional unity' means a unity of the three levels. Even though we focus our attention almost wholly in the physical structure, and the manipulative technique brings about physical changes, we are conscious all the time that changes are occuring on all three levels forming the functional unity — Spiritual, Psychological, Physical.

[1] E.g.; . the organism of man was originally and primarily patterned not for disease. neurosis and war, but for health, for whole organismic functioning throughout the species. (Trigant Burrow, The Neurosis of Man).

As we have already intimated, this work is not a mystical treatise nor theological thesis. It will suffice, therefore, if we give only a few indications (culled from Teachings in widely different parts of the world) of what we include as belonging to the Spiritual Structure of Man.

SPIRITUAL STRUCTURE OF MAN:

In the first place we affirm unhesitatingly that Man is not an animal, but represents a *different and higher* class of life. In support of this we quote the following:

1. We read in the first chapter of the Book of Genesis (vv 26,27.) that, after the creation of light, earth, water, plants, fishes, birds and animals, God said:

Let us make man in our own image, after our likeness. And God created man in his own image; in the image of God created he him; male and female he created them.

Later we read,

. . . and God saw everything that he had made, and behold it was very good.

Some of the immediately obvious implications are that, unlike animals,

Man has creative power;

Man has free will;

Man is able to be self-conscious;

Man has an aesthetic sense;

and so on.

We note there that in the Orthodox Chruch a careful distinction is made between 'Image' and 'Likeness'. S. John of Damascus wrote:

The expression *according to the image* indicates rationality and freedom, while the expression *according to the likeness* indicates assimilation to God through virtue.

Timothy Ware elucidates this:

"The Image, or to use the Greek term the *Icon,* of God signifies man's free will, his reason, his sense of moral responsibility — everything, in short, which makes him a *person.* But the image means more than that. It means that we are God's 'offspring'[1], His kin; it means that between us and Him there is a point of contact, an essential similarity. The gulf between creature and Creator is not impassable, for because we are in God's Image we can know God and have communion with Him. And if a man makes proper use of this faculty for communion with God, then he will become 'like' God, he will acquire the divine likeness; in the words of John Damascene, he will be 'assimilated to God through virtue'."

Thus we see that the Image denotes powers with which everyone is endowed, and one *never* loses the Image: but the 'Likeness', being a goal towards which everyone must strive, depends upon choice, or upon how he exercises his free will.

[1] Acts XVII, 28.

2. The Chi-Schara-Badgan doctrine of Tibet[1] postulates three Modes of existence[2], with three Steps in each Mode. Evolution begins with the manifestation of the Badgan Step of the Badgan Mode. This lowest is known as the Null Step, or the Space-Time Step. The next is the Schara of Badgan, the Thermic Radiation Step, with a Structure and Temperature sense. The Chi of Badgan is that which we in the West would call the Step of 'Inorganic' matter, or material bodies. With this Step is associated the Sense of Touch.

The Schara Mode has three Steps, its Badgan Step is that of Plants, with its Digestion Sense. The Schara of Schara represents a Step for which we have no western equivalent; it is called the Sex-differentiation Step, the related Sense being the Sex-Sense. We now come to the Chi, or highest Step of the Schara Mode: this is the Step of Animals, which of course includes birds, fishes, insects, etc., and has the related Sense of Smell.

The third Mode is called the Spirit Mode. On the *lowest* Step of this Mode is Man. Man represents the Badgan of Chi, having the special Sense of Taste, which has also the meaning Discrimination. Schara of Chi is the Step of Spirits. This is a difficult idea to translate as we do not recognise in the West any exact equivalent. The Sense associated with this Step is Sight. The highest Step of all, the Chi of Chi, is that of Principles with the associated Sense of Hearing and Speech. This, at its highest, should be taken to mean a Communication-Will-Understanding Sense.

Before we leave the Chi-Schara-Badgan ideas there is a further point of particular interest — the Lamas teach that every Step has within itself *all* the Steps. Those above are either latent or to some degree awakened and developing. All the Steps below are *developed and raised* appropriately.

Man has the distinction of being a microcosm.

3. Lorenz Oken, doctor of medicine and one-time professor of Natural History at the University of Zurich, presents the case[3] very clearly, logically and philosophically, showing how Man has spiritual characteristics and faculties, and belongs to a higher order than all other creatures.

Oken looks upon self-consciousness as a spiritual faculty possessed by Man but nōt by any creature below Man. Man, he says, is ratiocinative and aesthetic; he has a sense of Beauty and Art-forms, Colour, Music, Dance, Poetry, and Rhetoric. He distinguishes animal and plant thus:

1010 . . . a root grows, moves itself towards one spot, *not* because it there *seeks* for moisture, but because it is *affected* by the moisture which is there found. Were the moisture not to act upon it, it would wither.

1012 . . . the animal can move itself from *want* of stimulus. It moves itself to *seek* for, and thus from want of, nourishment, which consequently does not act upon it; the plant cannot, however, move itself owing to want of food, but only to die.

1013 *this is the essential and only conclusive distinction between animal and plant.*

[1] Tib.Med.Phil., Krazinski.
[2] cf. Dionysius the Areopagite, trans.C.E.Rolt, SPCK.
[3] Elements of Physiophilosophy, Ray Society, London 1847.

4. Alfred Korzybski differentiaties three classes of life[1], neatly confirming the distinctions made by Oken a hundred years earlier.

Plant Life represents the Chemical-binding class of life; so-called because plants convert sunlight and inorganic matter into organic matter.

Animal Life represents the Space-binding class of life. This means, according to Korzybski, that animals have the characteristic of freedom of voluntary movement in space. Plants do not have this freedom.

Man represents the Time-binding class of life by his ability to move in time. This does not, of course, mean moving in time in any science-fiction sense: man is able, by his mind, to relate past and present events with future possibilities. Again Man is, according to Korzybski, unique in his consciousness of abstracting in higher orders.

Korzybski's impact and influence on Western culture has been widespread and profound.

5. To illustrate the traditional chinese medical orientation concerning the spiritual structure of Man we quote extract from the Nei Ching:[2]

"The physician is different from the common man — those who are common and vulgar are not able to see ... the people know only how to live, they do not understand how to apply the five methods to get well from their diseases. The first method cures the spirit; the second gives knowledge of how to nourish the body. the third gives knowledge of the true effects of poisons and medicines; the fourth explains acupuncture and the use of the small and the large needle; the fifth tells how to examine and to treat the intestines, and the viscera, the blood and the breath. These five methods are drawn up together so that each has one that precedes it ...

... in order to make all acupuncture thorough and effective *one must first cure the spirit* ... when the spirit is calm and peaceful there will be a long life ... If one neglects the spirit the body becomes injured; therefore one should not be heedless of the nourishment and care of the spirit.

"What is the spirit?

"The spirit cannot be heard with the ear. The eye must be brilliant of perception and the heart must be open and attentive, and then the spirit is suddenly revealed through one's own consciousness. It cannot be expressed through the mouth; only the heart can express all that can be looked upon. If one pays close attention one may suddenly know it but one can just as suddenly lose this knowledge. But *Shen,* the spirit, becomes clear to man as though the wind has blown away a cloud."

Owing to elasticity of terms and meanings it is not easy to decide whether some items should be discussed under the heading Spiritual Structure, or under the heading Psychological Structure. There does seem to be a certain amount of unavoidable overlapping.

[1] Science & Sanity, An introduction to Non-aristotelian systems and General Semantics, Lakeville, Conn. U.S.A. Korzybski founded the Institute of General Semantics.
[2] Quoted in a paper read by Dr. Denis Lawson-Wood to the Acupuncture Association at the Congress 1973.

We should never forget that we ourselves, as organisms-as-a-whole-functioning-in-environments, must include in our own thinking 'Spiritual environments'.

We now pass on to say a few words about the Psychological Structure.

PSYCHOLOGICAL STRUCTURE OF MAN:

It has been said of Man that he is the only creature able to talk his way into difficulties that would otherwise not exist. It is also true of Man that he is able to think his way out of difficulties that would otherwise be insuperable.

One of the distinguishing characteristics of Man is that he is a symbol-forming and symbol-using creature. Although we do, of course, recognize that some of the higher vertebrates show response to symbols, their ability is very limited — so limited that, compared with Man, it can be looked upon as effectively non-existent.

What is perhaps the most significant difference between Man and Animal is illustrated by the influence of the symbol-using factor upon health. In Man, re-action to symbols in connection with their meanings affects colloidal structure and behaviour, bringing about physical and chemical changes. This will be at once clear if we point out that a dog shown a piece of paper with the words written on it 'Your puppy has just been run over and killed' will react quite differently from a woman who is handed a telegram informing her that her son has been killed in a road accident. The dog would neither faint, scream, nor burst into tears.

The environment, circumstances and conditions in which a person lives, influences his health and happiness; if this were not 'o there would be no point in slum clearance schemes, smoke abatement, anti-noise and anti-pollution propaganda. What we do need to bear in mind, as far as human beings are concerned *psychological environment* is a highly important factor. This factor includes language (national, class, professional or trade, and slang).

It is at least as important to control and reduce psychologically disturbing and destructive influences as it is to reduce adverse physical conditions.

We take it also to be a general valid precept that Vital Energy must not be wasted. This applies to psychic or mental energy as well as to physical.

We are not here concerned with *describing* psychological structure, but with *acknowledging* that it exists, and that there is a close link between psychological tensions and physical tensions, between psychological traumas and physical trauma. Any observant practitioner of the treatment herein outlined will certainly come across instances of this linkage in practically every case treated.

Over and over again we have had instances of worries, hates, resentments, doubts, guilt, fear, hunger and frustration *built-in* to the physical structure.

A physical dramatisation of a psychological pain or anxiety is often easier to bear than if it were not translated to the physical level, but remained a torment in the mind.

During treatment the *physical* immobility, scar, or manifestation will, on being dispersed, release the psychological manifestation from its physical prison so that it becomes available for re-assessment at the level to which it properly belongs. If psychological structure and functioning are ignored how can the practitioner be expected to deal with these eventualities? Happen they will.

Georg Groddek, M.D., wrote several lucid, informative and useful books showing linkages between physical and psychological states. As a massage and manipulative practitioner keenly interested in psycho-analysis he was able to combine his skills in a quite remarkable way. He saw nothing incongruous in treating physical ailments and diseases psychologically, or in treating psychological disturbances physically.

Wilhelm Reich, M.D., throws valuable light on the psyche-soma integrity and its treatment; his books should also be read.

In order to illustrate what we are talking about, we give an example of man's ability, through his faculty for abstracting in higher orders indefinitely, to change his psychological re-actions to either physical or psychological environments and circumstances — that is, if he chooses to use his human characteristic instead of remaining at the animal functioning level.

If a person's reaction to circumstances *which he can neither alter nor escape from* is one of anger — that is to say, if he is angry with those circumstances his behaviour towards them will tend to be destructive and of wasted effort. If he is unable to get beyond that anger his response is not better than animal response: because, in this instance, his ability to make higher order abstractions has shown severe limitation. This particular problem could be brought a step nearer to a satisfactory mature or creative solution simply by making the higher order abstraction of 'being angry with himself for being angry with circumstances beyond his control'. His attitude and behaviour then undergoes a significant change and his attention is drawn constructively towards that which he can alter and resolve *without suppression.*

Suppression or repression of an emotion is never equivalent to resolving it.

A suppressed or repressed anger may become built into the body tissues and manifest as some degree of arm and shoulder flexor shortening and immobility. *The anger becomes hidden in a muscle condition.* When that immobility has been manipulatively removed the emotion of anger will be available for re-assessment, and for a higher order abstraction to be made that will resolve the problem in a more mature human way.

The practitioner should be aware of such changes of level, and be prepared to deal with them. In general one could say that if the practitioner *understands* what is happening, the handling of the situation is relatively simple — often needing little more than a reassuring explanation.

PHYSICAL STRUCTURE OF MAN

There are several *physical* characteristics of Man that differentiate him markedly from all other life-forms. In Man the Animal is raised to a new level: four paragraphs from Oken's Physiophilosophy[1] summarise the

[1] Translated by Alfred Tulk, MRCS, London, Ray Society.

principal characteristics thus:

3575. In Man all the senses enter for first time into a state of perfect equiponderance or proportion. Skin naked, and therefore a perfect organ of feeling; feet and hands differently constructed for progression and manipulation; tongue and lips fleshy, while the latter have hitherto been only tegumental; all the kinds of teeth different, but still very similar, being of equal height and nearly equal size; nose elevated by its whole length from the face, and fleshy; ears oval, laid close against the head and having regular windings or convolutions; eyes directed forwards, with perfect eyelids, and moveable in all directions.

3576. Man by the upright walk obtains his character, namely, that of bodily freedom, for his hind feet take the place of all the four feet of the other animals, by which means the hands become free and can achieve all other offices, the feet alone serving to support the body.

He is the only creature that surveys with the axes of the eyes borne parallel with the most extensive horizon. All animals whose eyes look higher up or above the ground, as the Horse, Elephant, Ostrich, and such like creatures, have eyes directed sideways.

3577. With the freedom of the body has been granted also the freedom of the mind. Man sees everything, the whole universe, while the animals can only view individual parts thereof, two of these even invariably appearing different so that the images seen by them are never reduced to unity.

3578. There is only one human family, only one human genus, and only one species . . .

According to those who hold that Man has evolved or developed, it is reckoned that prehuman development, resulting in the erect posture, took a long time, and occurred in two distinct stages:

"First, there is the preparatory stage during which the early tarsoid quadruped was converted into an upright tree-living type with brachiating habits. (Eocine to early Miocene, 30,000,000 years) . . .

" . . . the Second great group of changes are those resulting from ground-living habits. These changes are restricted to the pre-human stock alone and result from the effect of gravity on a vertically supported body on the extended legs . . . The era began in the early Miocene and lasted to the present time (also about 30,000,000 years).[1]

When we realize that Man is the only creature able to oppose the palmar surfaces of the fingers (especially the last phalanges) with the palmar surface of the last phalange of the thumb; and that it is this very ability that makes it possible for him to manipulate minute parts and use fine tools (e.g. as does a watchmaker), we perhaps begin to wonder why Man has this gift, and where is he destined to go?

[1] Winthrop Morgan Phelps, D.M., Diagnosis & Treatment of Postural Defects. Charles C. Thomas 1932.

In his make-up Man has respresentative systems and functions of lower order. For example, Digestion, Assimilation, and Respiration are *Vegetative* functions which appeared for the first time in Plant life, but which are now, in Animals and Man, raised to a higher level.[1]

Before Plant life, however, there was inorganic or 'inert' matter. We do not like the generally current term 'inert', because Matter nevertheless 'grew', 'lived' and 'died' through gravity, cohering, chemical affinities and antagonisms, crystallization, and so on. This Earth Process or Structure function still goes on, and is raised to a new level in plant-life; again to a new level in animal life, and operates as the *cell-forming process; the appropriate system and tissues in Man are those of the Kyungrak System, the Bonghan Sanal Cell-Cycle, operating in the corpuscles and ducts traditionally known as the Acupuncture Meridians, Vessels, and Channels, and the Points.*[2]

Without wishing to tie ourselves down to technical exactness in use of words, we feel that the Chi-Schara-Badgan term 'Structural Sense' has considerable weight of logical thinking behind it. The Structure sense, appearing for the first time in 'earth' or inorganic material bodies, is raised to a new level in plant life where it operates ordering the structure function. When the plant function is raised to a new level in animal life the structure-function is raised with it, and has tissues and processes appropriate to it; just as the digestive, assimilative, and respiratory processes are raised and have organs, tissues, and processes appropriate to the new level.

An animal, embodying within itself Earth and Plant, is not a plant. *The characteristic tissues of animal life are muscle, bone, and nerve.*

Man, a new and higher life form, embodies within himself Earth, Plant, and Animal *raised to a new level.* Although Man has the lower functions, processes and organs, he is not an animal, nor a plant, nor an earth. The lowest man is higher than the uppermost ape because man belongs to a class higher.

We must stress this because we feel that the high destiny of Man is to be read, by those able to read it, where his physical structure is characteristically different from animal physical structure.

This brings us at once to the erect posture.

The erect posture has NOT been attained by the overwhelming majority of mankind. It is true that human beings approximate more or less to the upright stance: it is just this more-or-lessness that conceals from people the fact that their stance and dynamic posture is still inefficient, uneconomical, and wastes a very great deal of vital energy.

In our diagram, contrasting the normal upright with the supposed upright, it might be levelled at us that we have caricatured the poked forward head, rounded shoulders, protruding lower abdomen, and so on. A second and careful look at actual people around us in daily life will be quite revealing!

[1] Oken, passim.
[2] This placing by Dr. Denis lawson-Wood of the Chinese Ki energy system is here made for the first time. The placing is tentative, and suggestive of a line along which to research further.

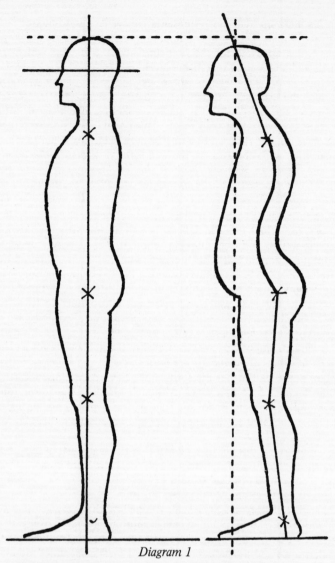

Diagram 1

Two important questions have now to be answered:

• 1. Why do people neither stand nor walk properly erect? 2. What significant physical and psychological consequences result from wrong posture?

The answers we arrive at to these questions will indicate what we ought to do, and what we can do about it.

Our first question is answered quite simply in a very few words. In general people do not either stand nor walk properly erect because they are not able to do so. We can give at least eight reasons for this inability: one or several of these factors may apply in each case.

14

1. **Affectation.** As an example of this we once had a case of a young man with an affected ape-like slouch, chin poked well forward, and arms hanging loosely at his side. He thought by this attitude that he was expressing 'real he-man grim determination'.

We have seen many cases of the head tilted slightly back, chin raised, and half-closed down-the-nose-looking eyes, intended to convey an air of lofty superiority, etc.

If followed for a sufficient length of time an affectation gets 'built in' so thoroughly that the person concerned becomes unable to undo it.

2. **Habit.** We are thinking here principally of the results of occupational strains and stresses, such as the rounded shoulders of so many clerical workers; the hip and sacro-iliac troubles caused by working long hours at a treadle, and so on.

3. **Psycho-logical dramatisations.** These may be closely akin to 'affectation' and 'habit', but not necessarily so. It is well known to psycho-analysts that there are the tell-tale postures – built-in expressions of fear, guilt, anger, etc. Even though a course of psychoanalytical treatment may bring the complexes to consciousness and clear them psychologically, the physical level dramatisation is not undone by 'realization'. Built-in problems and complexes more often than not will have to be physically treated *after* psycho-analysis.

Under this heading 'Dramatisations' we also include psycho-logical trauma, effects of shock, and so on.

4. **Clothes.** Corsets and wasp-waists are rather out of date these days. Nevertheless restrictive clothing is still an important factor. The two worst offenders we can think of are Shoes & Socks. Any intelligent observer is able to see how high heels throw the whole body out of alignment and cause unnatural shortening of some muscle groupings. What, however, is not quite so obvious is the effect on the very young of socks that are too tight. Continuous compression of an infant's feet, for eight or even up to twelve hours a day, is a more serious danger than shoes that are too small. Socks that are too tight cause contracted feet, clawed toes, or drawn up toes, and from these inevitably follows awkward standing.

5. **Injury.** Some conditions arising out of injuries we can do very little about. A case comes to mind of an upper limb amputation at the shoulder. In the course of years the development of the muscles of the other shoulder had pulled the upper part of the spine out of alignment. We could see no way of counteracting this sideways pull. Fortunately not all injuries are as serious as that.

There are ever so many injuries ordinarily looked upon as too trivial to do much about; and, of course, there are bone fractures where, as we have so often been told by our clients, the 'doctor' has instructed, "Dont allow any quack to massage it".

Wherever there has been a fracture, laceration, cuts or bruises *there will be scar tissue.* All scar tissue causes some degree of immobility or obstruction to full normal functioning therefore, as soon as a 'healing' has occurred, as much scar tissue as possible should, in our view, be dispersed. Massage must be done intelligently.

6. **Deformity.** Postural defects due to congenital deformity may not be suitable for the present method of treatment: one must not expect this technique to accomplish unlimited miracles. Nevertheless there will be instances where, although the posture will not be alterable, there will always be room for greater relaxation, economy and improved functioning. Everyone, however seriously deformed or handicapped, must breathe — and breathing can almost always be improved.

7. **Illness.** When a postural defect is due to the sequelae of an illness, e.g, asthma, t.b., rheumatic fever, etc., assessment needs to be made by a competant practitioner to make sure that there is no contra-indication to massage treatment. There are times when scar tissue acts as an isolator of infection: scar tissue of this nature should not be disturbed.

8. **Chain-accumulation.** Although this term is not a technical one to be found in medical dictionaries, it is a useful descriptive heading under which to include an incredibly wide variety of postural defects due, not to one single cause, but to a succession of minor causes. Each of the minor causes, taken singly, appears trivial and insignificant, but when their *totality* is taken into account the factor takes on importance.

Every bruise however slight, every cut from earliest childhood will tend to leave *some* scar tissue even though minuscule. Any scar causes an obstruction to the flow of some fluid or an immobility in the area *however small*. There are places where a very small scar or adhesion can cause an apparently disproportionate disruption simply because of its position; while quite a large scar may appear to give little inconvenience, if any, again on account of its location.

Our second question, What significant physical and psychological consequences result from wrong posture? This again can be answered quite simply: Energy and vitality will be wasted.

If, for example, instead of maintaining a relaxed upright balanced posture, the posture has to be maintained by muscle tensions, energy is being used up that would not be being used if there were not that particular set of tensions. Muscle tensions never involve one muscle only: muscles always work in pairs, a protagonist with its antagonist.

A continuously tense muscle inhibits flow of *all* fluids whether blood, lymph, or the Ki energy fluid (now known in parts of the Far East as Bonghan Fluid). This is of importance to the acupuncture practitioner who may be puzzled why, sometimes, an energy deficiency is not balanced by the 'supply' action with a needle at the indicated point.

If energy that is now being wasted can be redirected so that it is no longer wasted but is either stored or creatively used, then that person's *quality* of living will be improved.

ATTITUDE TO THE CLIENT.

It should not be necessary to tell a practitioner what his attitude ought to be towards the client. Indeed for the majority of our readers these words will be superfluous; but as an increasing number of conventionally trained medical practitioners become interested in this kind of work[1]

[1] Preventative Naturopathy and Acupuncture.

it is necessary to remind them that this Progessive Vitality treatment is NOT a therapy. That is to say, it is not an instance of a sick person being treated according to theories he would have little chance of understanding; nor is it an instance of a patient, for his own good and the 'doctor's ' convenience, being kept in ignorance of what he is given, what it is given for, and what the chances are of it doing any good.

Anyone intelligent enough to realize that he is not ill in the ordinary sense, but at the same time realizes that there is, nevertheless, a great deal of room for improvement, and has come to you for that very reason, deserves co-operative understanding.

Almost anyone you question on the topic would agree that, even in his own case, posture could be improved; and that better posture could mean greater efficiency, energy economy and, therefore, a better chance of remaining in good health.

Telling your client beforehand what it is proposed to do can make the doing of it a lot easier, and more beneficial to him. Enlist his co-operation by telling him: "This is not so much something I am going to do to you, as something we are going to achieve together".

It is worthwhile spending a little time explaining the process and talking about it.

Encourage your client to talk freely to you, by all means; but also tactfully encourage him to recognise the value of experiencing in silence that which is happening on non-verbal levels. Endless superficial chatter will get you nowhere: neither will suppression of important information.

Your client needs to be reassured that whatever is told to you is automatically treated as confidential. Even more important is that you listen *without* condemnation or judgement. You yourself must be fully convinced from experience that judgement includes both blame and praise. If some items are warmly praised by you, your client soon has a good idea that items of the opposite sort would probably meet with your disapproval and, therefore, are best left unsaid.

Accept whatever is told to you. Accept it with understanding and, if any criticism is to be made, *let* the client himself make the criticism.

You may well wonder why this is so important when, after all, we are doing physical manipulations not conducting a psycho-analysis!

Remember what we said earlier on: Release of physical tensions usually means that at the same time there is a related release of psycho-logical or emotional tie-ups. Your client must understand that there is no *need* for him to reveal any problem or tension to you at all, but if he does his Privacy and Confidences will be one hundred per cent respected.

The practitioner MUST abide by this absolutely.

Since our Number One treatment is primarily concerned with breathing we think it advisable to say a few words about breathing before we go on to a detailed description of the 'number one manipulations'.

BREATHING.

All the time we are alive cells are being made, working, dying, disintegrating and being replaced. In other words, living is a continuous process of rejuvenation or replacement. Good health may optimally be expected when proper necessary cell-formation is unobstructed, and the general circumstances prevail wherein there is full availability in both quantity and quality of the right material.

One of the essential materials is oxygen which, from birth onwards, is obtained from the air we breathe. We get a great deal more that is vital from breathed air than oxygen, but we do not need to itemise other essentials. It is sufficient to look upon oxygen as representative of all we need from air. Although breathing is such a vital process, far too little thought and attention is given to it.

How often do we breathe? How much do we take in each time? Although Tables of rates and volume will be found in any good handbook of physiology for students, it will not come amiss to set down a few facts and figures to show what the average 'healthy' adult does, his breathing rate and volume, and how different it could be.

The total volume of air, some of which can in certain circumstances be breathed in and out through nose, mouth, and air passages into the lungs is known as *Vital Capacity*. In adults this averages between 3000 cc and 4000 cc. In ordinary quiet breathing, however, the amount breathed in and out each time is not more than 15% of this total. The air actually breathed in and out each time is known as *Tidal Air;* this averages somewhere between 400 cc and 500 cc.

BUT 150 cc of tidal air is *dead* air. This 150 cc is *dead* because although breathed in through nose or mouth, it NEVER reaches the lungs; similarly the last 150 cc of tidal air breathed out of the lungs NEVER goes out of the nose or mouth. The *dead* air is that which fills the upper air passages and bronchial tubes. (see diagram).

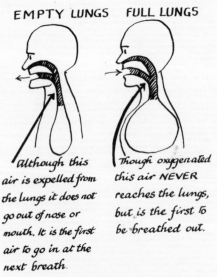

EMPTY LUNGS   FULL LUNGS

although this air is expelled from the lungs it does not go out of nose or mouth. It is the first air to go in at the next breath.

Though oxygenated this air NEVER reaches the lungs, but is the first to be breathed out.

Diagram 2

18

Suppose we take an example of a typical adult male who, in quiet breathing has a tidal capacity of 450 cc and a breathing rate of 18 per minute. 450 cc tidal air minus 150 cc dead air leaves 300 cc of active air per breath. Multiply this by 18; we thus calculate that 5400 cc of active or oxygenated air reaches his lungs per minute.

He can increase this considerably. We notice that if his *Vital* capacity is 3500 there is a difference between Total and Tidal. 3500–450=3050: What happens to that?

About half, i.e., 1500cc, can be drawn into the lungs in the deepest breathing: this is called *Complemental air.* The remaining reserve of 1500 cc is called *Supplemental air,* which may be breathed out.

Tidal + Complemental + Supplemental = Vital Capacity.

There is a residual 1600 cc which is always in the lungs and cannot be breathed out.

Now his oxygen or breath intake per minute can be increased *either* by speeding up the breathing rate, leaving the tidal amount unchanged, or by deeper breathing.

It can quickly be shown that increased breathing rate is uneconomical: so much so that it is a rather stupid angle of approach. The same amount of dead and useless air has to be pumped in and out at every breath; why, then, do twice as much useless work, using more energy to do it? Surely it would be more sensible to breathe more *deeply* even if one has to breathe more slowly!

If breathing is shallow enough, that is to say if the tidal air went down to 150 cc the person, in spite of breathing, would die, because no oxygenated air would ever reach the lungs. It would not matter how rapidly he breathed, if he breathed only dead air, he would die.

Lets make up a table for comparisons.

A	B	C	D	E	F
Rate per minute	Volume per breath.	Dead air per breath	Volume per minute	Dead air per minute	Active air per minute
18	450 cc	150 cc	8100 cc −	2700 cc =	5400 cc
9	900 cc	150 cc	8100 cc −	1350 cc =	6750 cc
6	1350 cc	150 cc	8100 cc −	900 cc =	7200 cc

Note that in this Table we have decreased the rate and increased the volume per breath so that the volume per minute remains the same. Slower and deeper breathing is more efficient in spite of (in this instance) the total volume per minute remaining unaltered.

We now come to an important though unfortunate fact of life: all too frequently there is a wide difference between a person's *potential* vital capacity and the *actual or operative* vital capacity.

19

For one reason or another a person *may not be able to breathe as deeply as he should be able to breathe.* In the majority of cases this inability can be almost wholly overcome.

As we have pointed out, full and free movement may be severely restricted by the cumulative effect of a multitude of minor injuries, each too small to have registered as more than a bruise or knock, but each one of which has left *some* scar tissue or adhesion. The totality, an accumulation over a period perhaps of twenty, thirty, or more years, represents a formidable hindrance. Habit, shock, physical injury, psychological trauma, illnesses and diseases of one kind and another *leave their mark* on the body somewhere. These marks are not all indelible! Breathing can be improved by dispersion of scars, adhesions, immobilities and so on that restrict the breathing apparatus

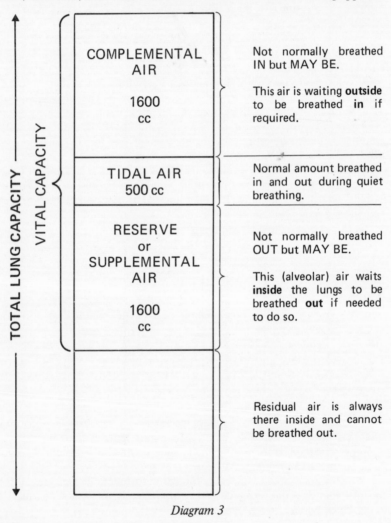

Diagram 3

20

Consider next the diagram showing capacity proportions, and the average positioning of the Tidal band about half-way or with as much Complemental as Supplemental air.

When, at the commencement of the first treatment you watch your subject's breathing you will be trying to assess where his 'tidal-air band' is placed. Does this subject first need to take more IN or to let more OUT? You will arrive at your assessment by watching and feeling the range of movement of the rib-cage and diaphragm, noting where the restrictions are. We have had a case where the tidal-band of 500 cc was so near the top of the column (diagram) that there was almost no complemental air, but a huge and quite disproportionate supplemental air. It was this particular case that emphasized to us the need to note whereabouts the client's tidal-band is operating. This particular client's problem was that he could not breathe OUT; the physical difficulty was a dramatization of a psychological trauma he had in infancy more than seventy years before he came to us. This problem was resolved in due course and our client lived a further twelve years enjoying excellent health almost to the last.

In this work we are NOT suggesting any range of breathing exercises, disciplines, or breath-control disciplines. Without the guidance and direction of an expert some breath-control disciplines can be dangerous.

TREATMENT ROOM & WORKING SURFACE.

We assume the availability of facilities normally found in any practitioner's treatment rooms: Somewhere for the client to be interviewed; Somewhere for the client to undress; toilet for the client's use; washing facilities for the operator. In the treatment room itself, which need be only quite small; the only essential item of equipment, if one is thinking in primitive terms, is a clean surface upon which the client stands, sits, or lies down.

This need be no more than a sheet a yard wide by two and a half yards long. We recommend, however, that a few refinements and additions be made: A sheet of foam rubber, not more than an inch thick, be placed inside a loose cover, and the client's 'contact-sheet' is placed on top of this. In lieu of foam rubber, several thicknesses of blanket material will be found just as suitable.

A few firm pillows or cushions are helpful in supporting the client according to position required.

We found that many patients do not feel at ease at floor level, and prefer to be on a table or couch. We have also noticed that, in general, therapists do not find it easy to massage, manipulate, or adjust, at floor level. They too prefer a treatment table or couch. The ordinary physiotherapy table, or osteopathy and cheiropractic couch is quite useless for Progressive Vitality treatments.

The surface must be flat and wide enough. The table we had made for our own treatment room was very solidly made of wood; the dimensions are shown in the illustration. The hinged section was made to support a sitting patient.

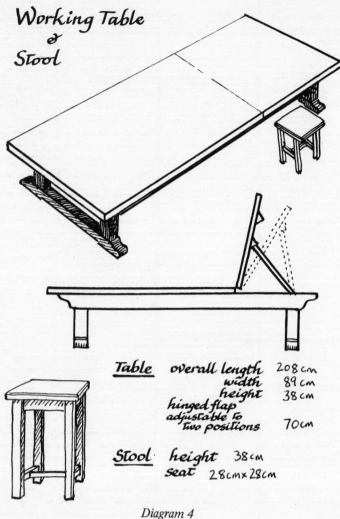

Working Table & Stool

Table	overall length	208 cm
	width	89 cm
	height	38 cm
	hinged flap adjustable to two positions	70 cm

Stool	height	38 cm
	seat	28 cm x 28 cm

Diagram 4

If one is working without a table, and using the floor level throughout, the client for some operations would be propped with his back against one of the walls.

If a table is to be used, then a stool about the same height is needed for the operator to sit on (illustration).

For some operations the therapist will find it more convenient to kneel on the floor alongside the couch.

MANIPULATIONS AND MASSAGES.

What are we actually trying to do? When we say we want to 'free an area', what exactly do we mean?

An illustration which we have often used in lectures, talks, and discussions, could quite usefully be repeated here. The reader must remember, however, that no simile is fully adequate, especially if it involves comparing a living circumstance with an inanimate one. Nevertheless there are certain mechanical principles which can be so demonstrated.

Suppose, for example, we have a short length of rope, cord or string (AB) with a part of it (CD) thoroughly impregnated with glue or gum so that all the fibres of this section are matted together and there is no longer any flexibility there.

Diagram 5

However often or however hard one pulls at the two ends A and B the section CD will NOT be loosened or freed from its gumming up. If, instead of string, we have 'gummed-up' muscle fibres the same reasoning applies and no amount of pulling by exercises will ever free CD.

Going back to the 'string' analogy, we can quite easily test out several kinds of movement that *will* separate out the fibres and restore flexibility.

1. **Bending** backwards and forwards, up and down, or side to side. This would best be done by holding CD firmly at D (or C) to make the first bends at D (or C) by moving DB (or AC). Once the loosening has started the bending may safely involve a wider range of movement, and be more rapid.

2. **Rolling** across the direction of the fibres while pressing on a hard or firm surface. This can easily be done with the string by pressing it against the table surface. Muscle fibres may be pressed against a bone to be rolled; or squeezed between thumb and fingers with a 'cigarette-rolling' action.

3. **Pressure** in the direction of the fibres, starting at one end of the 'gummed area'. This has a forcing apart effect, rather like driving a wedge along. This can be extremely painful. So indeed can the previous two ways; but, if done at a proper speed, the pain element can be considerably reduced.

We aim to eliminate painful treatment altogether: and *this can be done:* but in order to do so a completely different orientation is needed.

Going back to the string fibre analogy, we have so far only suggested freeing the fibres by *breaking up glue that has set.* We now have to envisage the possibilities of un-setting or dissolving the glue, and either washing it away to get rid of it, or to change it in some way so that it does not re-set.

Our new orientation then, towards living fibres, is that we shall have to become 'colloid-gel-and-sol' minded. It is amazingly simple to understand and to work the new technique, it is absolutely safe, and painless. A few words about colloids, colloidal structure and behaviour will make it quite clear. We quote from Korzybski's *Science & Sanity*, Chapter IX, on Colloidal behaviour:—

When we take a piece of some material and subdivide it into smaller pieces, we cannot carry on this process indefinitely. At some stage of this process the bits become so small that they cannot be seen with the most powerful microscope. At a further stage, we should reach a limit of the subdivision that the particles can undergo without losing their chemical character. Such a limit is called the molecule. The smallest particle visible in the microscope is still about one thousand times larger than the largest molecule. So we see that between the molecule and the smallest visible particle there is a wide range of sizes. Findlay calls these the 'Twilight zone of matter'; and it was Oswald, I believe, who called it the 'world of neglected dimensions'.[1]

This world of neglected dimensions is of particular interest to us, because in this range of subdivision or smallness we find very peculiar forms of behaviour —life included—which are called 'colloidal behaviour'.

. . . In general, a colloid may be described as a 'system' consisting of two or more phases. The commonest represent emulsions or suspensions of fine particles in a gaseous, liquid, or other medium, the size of the particles grading from those barely visible microscopically to those of molecular dimensions. These particles may be either homogenous solids, or liquids, or solutions themselves of a small percentage of the medium in an otherwise homogenous complex. Such solutions have one characteristic in common; namely, that the suspended materials may remain almost indefinitely in suspension, because the tendency to settle, due to gravity, is counteracted by some other factor tending to keep the particles suspended. In the main, colloidal behaviour is not dependent upon the physical state or chemistry of the finely subdivided materials or of the medium.

. . . Materials which exhibit this special colloidal behaviour are always in a very fine state of subdivision, so that the ratio of *surface exposed* to *volume of material* is very large.

. . . The smaller the colloidal particles, the closer we come to molecular and atomic sizes. Since we know atoms represent electrical *structures,* we should not be surprised to find that, in colloids, surface energies and electrical charges become of fundamental importance, as by necessity all surfaces are made up of electrical charges. The surface energies operating in finely grained and dispersed systems are large, and in their tendency for a minimum, every two particles or drops tend to become one; because, while the mass is not altered by this change, the surface of one larger particle or drop is less than the surface of two

---

[1] As we have understood so far the discoveries of the Bong Han team the Chinese Acupuncture meridians, points, and energy belong somewhere in this 'world of neglected dimensions' – D. Lawson-Wood.

smaller ones – an elementary geometrical fact. Electrical charges have the well-known characteristic that like repels like and attracts the unlike. In colloids, the effect of these factors is of a fundamental, yet opposite, character. The surface energies tend to unite the particles, to coagulate, flocculate or precipitate them. In the meanwhile the electrical charges tend to preserve the state of suspension by repelling the particles from each other. On the predominance or intensity of one or other of these factors, the instability or the stability of a suspension depends."

The process of the dispersed phase, coagulating, is called the 'ageing' of the colloid. When coagulation is complete and irreversible the colloid is dead. Some coagulating processes are reversible and the changes are changes in viscosity.

The dispersed state is called 'sol' and the coagulated state is called 'gel'.

All life is found in the colloidal form; and there are many areas of 'gel' which have been in that state of 'gel' for a very long time and unlikely to do other than continue the slow ageing process *but which are nevertheless reversible if energy of the right kind can be applied.*

There are important differences between organic and inorganic colloidal behaviour, which we need not elaborate here. Our present concern is the realisation that in our manipulations and massages we are dealing in the main with immobilities caused by too much 'gel' where there should be more 'sol': or we could say that we are dealing with tissues, layers, sheaths, fibres, etc, adhering which should not be so 'gummed'. As indicated above, much of these immobilities can be separated by physical force, even though the force be quite gently applied. The adhesions may also be loosened by turning 'gel' into 'more sol', so that the structures may easily be manipulated into position, or will even of themselves re-instate themselves in their proper place as soon as they are free to do so.

The problem now is reduced to finding a suitable technique for controlling colloidal balance: we have to enquire, What factors can affect colloidal structure of *living protoplasm?*

Korzybski lists the four main factors able to disturb colloidal equilibrium, thus:

(1) Physical, as, for instance, X-rays, radium, light, ultra-violet rays, cathode rays, etc.
(2) Mechanical, such as friction, puncture, etc.[1]
(3) Chemical, such as tar, paraffin, arsenic, etc.
(4) Biological, such as microbes, parasites, spermatozoa, etc.

Factors (3) and (4) do not concern us in this form of treatment: but the first two factors do. The physical factor 'heat', chiefly applied through the natural warmth of the human hand, and the mechanical factors 'pressure, tension, torsion, etc', applied by fingers, knuckles, hands, and at times by elbow, are clearly important. But, as Korzybski points out, *in man there is another fifth potent factor; namely, semantic reactions.* This means *reactions to words and/or symbols in connection with their meaning.*

[1] also pressure, tension, torsion, etc.

25

The practitioner's will, intention, attention, and visualisation, in conjunction with physical and mechanical factors can and do profoundly affect colloidal equilibrium.

This is one of the principal reasons why it is so strongly recommended that the operator concentrate on what he is doing, and does not chatter superficially. Listen to what the person being treated has to say, yes! But that is very different from going through the physical motions with the hands and fingers while the mind and tongue wander on superficial irrelevancies.

How 'intention' works we do not know. Whether 'intention' affects the colloidal equilibrium of the area being treated by causing some differences in outflow of electricity through the finger-tips, or by means of any other outflow of 'rays', 'emanations' or 'energy', we do not know; and we do not know of anyone who claims to know. We have, however, experienced the fact of manipulating muscle areas ordinarily looked upon as inaccessible to massage and manipulation, such as the upper attachments of the psoas major. These areas we have reached and manipulated by steady, slow, patient pressure, coupled with intention.

Once the technique has been experienced it will be sufficiently understood to make it work predictably.

These few words should help that experience: Have a clear picture in your mind of what the muscle and other structure should be at the place you are working; *Let* the fingers sink into the flesh to the right depth *when the flesh is ready;* Do not use brute force, nor make any sudden or jerking movements.

Remember too, whether you are receiving a fee or not, it is a great privilege for you to have skill and opportunity to work on and with another human being: Respect that privilege.

TREATMENT SESSIONS

Session 1.

The whole course of Progressive Vitality Treatment will take in all about eight hours, which can conveniently be done in eight sessions. In rare cases two additional treatment sessions may be needed between numbers seven and eight.

The first session is by far the longest and may quite easily take up to an hour and a half to complete. Fortunately this first session is made up of two distinct parts, so, if absolutely necessary, it may be divided into two sessions. We have not had to make this division ourselves, and we recommend that the whole of the first session be completed at one visit. Where possible photographic records of 'Before' and 'After' each session should be kept.

The two parts have the following goals:

Part 1. To increase active lung capacity, increasing oxygenation.

Part 2. To give greater mobility to the pelvis.

There is a third, but not long, part which deals with the preliminary freeing of the neck musculature. This is taken at the end of the second part; it is not long enough to justify separating it from this first session.

PART 1. Look at the Subject, front view, side view, back view, focussing attention on *how the Subject breathes,* and whether *he is standing relaxed.* Note to what extent, in your estimation, this person's breathing is restricted by posture, or the posture is a result of faulty or restricted breathing.

The Subject is then asked to lie down on his back and to settle in a comfortable *relaxed* position. He is instructed to draw his knees up *dragging his heels.* You may be surprised how few people will carry out this simple instruction correctly at the first time of asking.

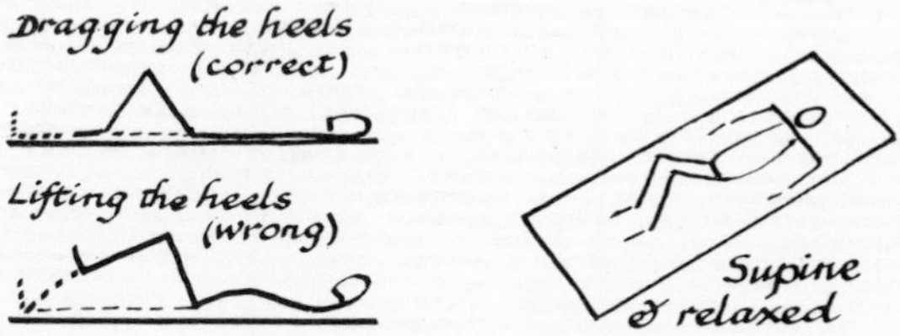

Diagram 6

If the instruction is correctly followed the movement will be relatively effortless: the two principal muscles necessary to perform this movement are the psoas (major and minor) and the iliacus. These are the *proper* flexors of the thighs. We are aiming for a supine position that is relaxed; this we shall not get if far more muscles than necessary are used, leaving the body (at the end of the movement) awkwardly tensed.

What so often happens on being given the instruction the Subject lifts, or tries to lift, both heels off the floor or working surface. The immediate effect of this is that it is now no longer a question of tightening the muscles that will flex the thighs but, in addition, the weight of the legs has to be carried. The rectus abdominis tightens to prevent the pelvis tilting forwards; and nearly all the abdominal muscles (including the diaphragm) will tighten to create enough internal abdominal pressure to keep the spine from arching. All the deep layers of the spinal musculature also come into operation to maintain spinal integrity (prevent it buckling). As far as we are able we aim to help the Subject towards *economical,* and therefore correct, use of the muscles thereby saving energy and, as it so happens, achieve graceful relaxed movements. Movement becomes graceful when the proper muscles are used in the correct order.

Few people are able to lie supine with the legs fully extended without experiencing a feeling of strain and tension. We need to have the Subject as relaxed as he is able to get *at this stage;* that is to say, *without* compensatory held tensions that are trying to relieve the strain of extension at hip and knees.

Ask the client to breathe deeply. Watch carefully and note which side appears to be the more restricted. The two halves of the rib-cage rarely exactly balance. Make a point of asking him to take special notice of how his breathing feels to him because, you tell him, 'When this session is finished, it will never feel the same again'.

Start work on the *better* side. The reason for this being that the second side will tend to be easier than the first, because the second side, in some way,

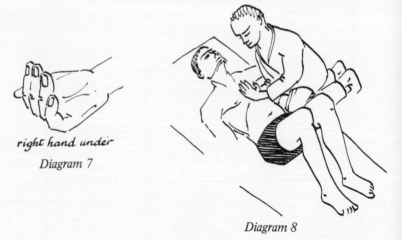

right hand under

Diagram 7

Diagram 8

28

seems to learn from the other. We will assume, for the sake of descriptive clarity, that we have chosen to work first on the client's left side.

The first manipulative operation is to begin freeing the ribs *at and close to* their dorsal attachments AND freeing the deepest layers of the post-vertebral muscles. Though small these deep muscles have a very important function: on them depends the integrity of the spine.

These structures (muscles, articulations, etc) are reached and worked on by placing the right hand underneath the patient, allowing his own weight to take your flexed fingers into the appropriate areas. Begin at the level of the

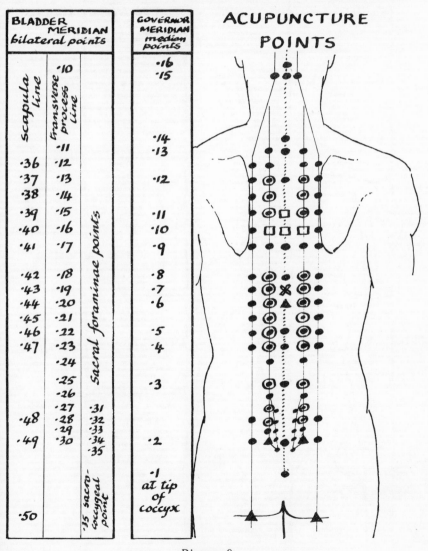

Diagram 9

29

articulation of the seventh cervical and first thoracic vertebrae, close to the spinous processes. The left hand will rest *lightly* on the client's chest (to *feel* the front end of the rib) near the manubrium (or sternum as the case may be), for it will be here that the operator will best be able to 'sense' what is happening at the spinal articulation.

Let the fingers sink into the flesh right to the deepest muscle layer, the intertransversarii and rotatores, and to the muscles (close to the vertebro-costal articulations) which are directly involved in breathing, the levatores costarum and the serrati posterior-superiores. (see illustrations)

Skeleton & deepest layer of post-vertebral muscles

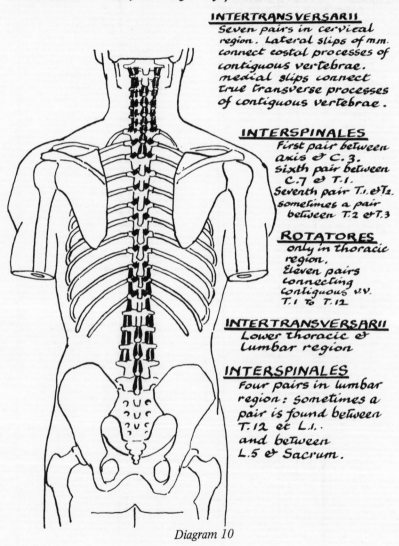

INTERTRANSVERSARII
Seven pairs in cervical region. Lateral slips of mm. connect costal processes of contiguous vertebrae. medial slips connect true transverse processes of contiguous vertebrae.

INTERSPINALES
First pair between axis & C.3. sixth pair between C.7 & T.1. Seventh pair T.1 & T.2. sometimes a pair between T.2 & T.3

ROTATORES
only in thoracic region. Eleven pairs connecting contiguous v.v. T.1 to T.12

INTERTRANSVERSARII
Lower thoracic & lumbar region

INTERSPINALES
Four pairs in lumbar region: sometimes a pair is found between T.12 et L.1. and between L.5 & Sacrum.

Diagram 10

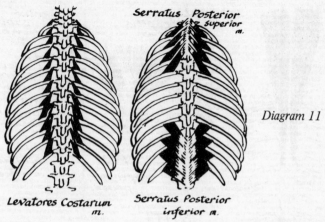

Serratus Posterior superior m.

Diagram 11

Levatores Costarum m.

Serratus Posterior inferior m.

The operator, especially at this stage, is NOT expected to be able to distinguish all the layers and individual slips with his fingertips, naming each muscle in each layer; but he should *know* what is there, and be able to feel whether or not there is free movement: he should, too, be able to feel clean bone contours. The illustrations are not intended to teach a student where

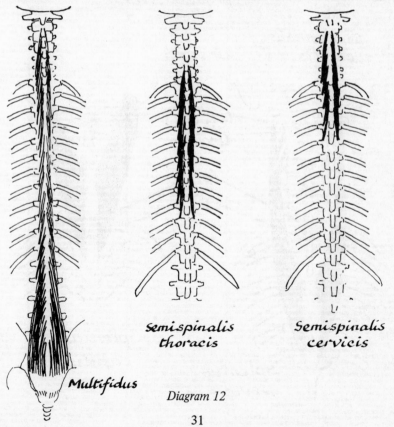

semispinalis thoracis

semispinalis cervicis

Multifidus

Diagram 12

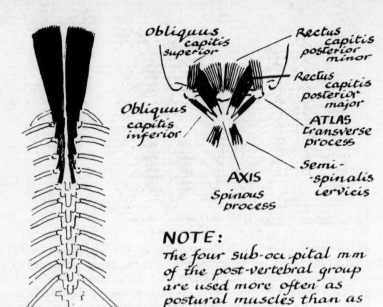

Obliquus capitis superior

Rectus capitis posterior minor

Rectus capitis posterior major

ATLAS transverse process

Obliquus capitis inferior

Semi-spinalis cervicis

AXIS
Spinous process

NOTE:

The four sub-occipital mm of the post-vertebral group are used more often as postural muscles than as prime-movers.

Semispinalis capitis

Diagram 13

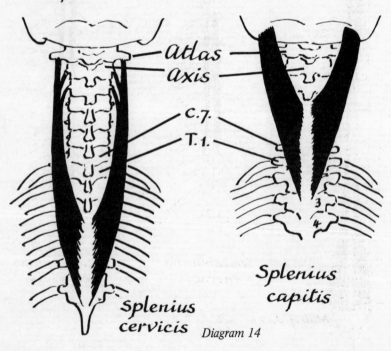

Atlas

Axis

C.7.

T.1.

3

4

Splenius cervicis

Splenius capitis

Diagram 14

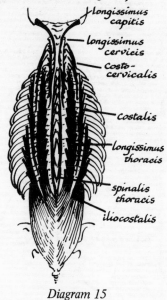

Sacro-spinalis group

longissimus capitis

longissimus cervicis

costo-cervicalis

costalis

longissimus thoracis

spinalis thoracis

iliocostalis

Diagram 15

muscles are, but to *remind* the operator. The tips of the fingers are used to separate, liberate, and clean: the intention must be focussed strongly on doing just that. Work at each articulation in this way as far as T9 or T10.

Now work on the axilla. With the palm of the right hand flat on the Subject's ribs push and press the finger ends up into the attachment of the pectoralis. The palm of the left hand is placed on the pectoralis and the muscle gently lifted with both hands. The fingers and/or side of the hand are used to ease the teres, remember, this first part of the first session is NOT the 'shoulder-girdle' session, and our focus throughout this first part is on the breathing structures.

In spite of our general principle *Periphery to Core* or *Outermost layers to Inner or Deeper layers* some of the outer muscle layers and large groups are only dealt with quite lightly in this first session; we have to do a certain amount of preliminary freeing in order to get at the rib-cage. Our *present concentration* is at or close to the vertebro-costal articulations, the intercostals, and the diaphragm.

Still working on the client's left side the intercostals are tackled working from the vertebrae towards the axillary line. The objective is to ensure that the fibres of each intercostal muscle are free, and also that the muscle layers themselves are not 'stuck to one-another'.

The finger tips will be firmly pressed into the muscle origins and drawn along the lower edge of each rib *with the intention* of cleaning the bone and separating what should be separate and free. Similarly finger-tips, ends of first phalanges, or even knuckles are drawn along the upper edges of the ribs at the intercostal muscle insertion.

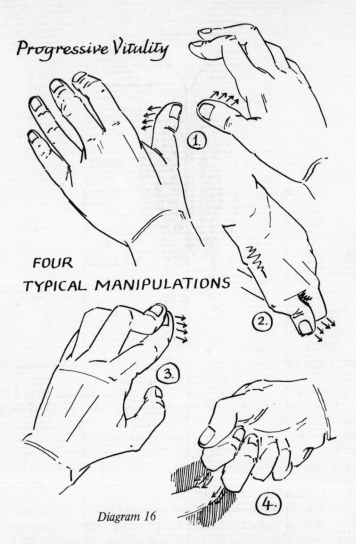

Progressive Vitality

FOUR

TYPICAL MANIPULATIONS

Diagram 16

DO NOT HURRY. It is better to cover the same ground two or three times slowly and without causing pain than once heavily, quickly and painfully. Long before we have finished freeing between the ribs of this first side we should be able to see that elasticity is in fact becoming restored and the thoracic cage becoming a flexible structure.

When the spaces between the ribs have been done, (and the costal cartilages of course), attention is given to the *diaphragm.*

We are only concerned at this stage with the muscle fibres which arise from the costal margin and from the xyphoid process. The vertebral fibres which arise from the lumbar vertebrae and from the arcuate ligaments *we shall not be able to organise until* the upper attachments of the psoas muscles have been freed: this will not be until Session Five.

34

It is usual to start at the xyphoid and work away from the centre line. Thumb and forefinger, or thumb and distal end and forefinger first phalange will be found the most efficient manipulative technique to clear clean and free the anterior costal border. Do not try to do it all in one heavy sweep. Use short strokes many times repeated until it is possible to get the fingers just under the cartilage the whole width of the rectus abdominis insertion.

When this has been done, the Subject is told to take a few deep breaths, and to tell you what it now feels like. *There will be a noticeable difference between the two sides.* The Subject usually makes a remark or exclamation indicating that the difference is both felt and appreciated, sufficiently to be quite eager for the other side to be done to match. The operator should himself be able to see the difference, and here and there make a few adjustments until that first half expands and contracts smoothly and harmoniously.

The second half of the thorax is now done in exactly the same order. Both halves of the rib-cage must be completed before anything is done in the pelvic region or to the lower limbs.

PART 2. The Subject is now instructed to bring his knees up on the abdomen and rest his hands on the knees, but not with the fingers interlaced as he may be tempted to do, as this would tend to conceal restrictions in the adductor structure.

The operator, with his own hands on the Subject's knees, rocks the knees two or three times towards the stomach. This is to test the mobility and range of movement at the sacrum and lower lumbar vertebrae.

The operator tests the function and range of movement around the head of the femur, and the mobility of the muscles that hold the femur in towards the sacrum. This test is made by lightly tossing the Subject's knees from side to side until the legs fall to one side. The side with the greater range of movement, and therefore the better side, will now be uppermost. Having let go of his knees the Subject will let his arms relax comfortably out of the way. A firm pillow should be used to give support to the head.

We need to remember that this can only be a preliminary freeing of the muscle origins and insertions at the hip joint: some muscles we shall not attempt to reach at all in this first hour as, for example, the femoral attachments of the psoas major and minor and the iliacus which, although inserting at the lesser trochanter, lie too deep to reach at this stage. The psoas muscle *origins* may justly be said to be the principal objective of this whole course of treatment, but it will not be until the fourth and fifth session that we shall be able to organise the psoas. It will also be realised that owing to the interweaving of the crura and upper attachments of the psoas we will not be able finally to free the diaphragm until the fifth session *after* the psoas has been freed.

Our work at this session is on the peripheral or near peripheral structures at and around the great trochanter and upper two thirds of the lateral aspect of the thigh. We work on the tensor fasciae latae, the sartorius (at its origin only, at the anterior superior iliac spine) and at the origin of the quadriceps femoris.

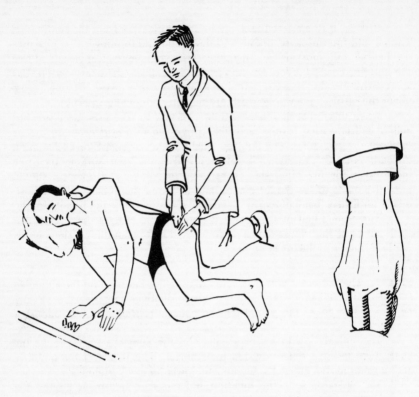

Diagram 17   Diagram 18

We do not manipulate the medial femoral muscles (gracilis, pectineus, adductor longus, brevis and magnus) until session number four: and the main body of the gluteal musculature will not be worked over until number six. But we do, at this session, clean the femoral attachments of the gluteus maximus, medius and minimus, piriformis, obturator internus, the gemelli, and the quadratus femoris.

The manipulative movements will principally be very deep pressure. The operator uses the weight of his own body to get in sufficiently around the trochanter. DO NOT RUSH IT. Unless the pressure is applied gradually and sensitively the Subject can be given a deal of unnecessary pain.

Work down the ilio-tibial tract to just above the knee articulation.

While on this part of the session it is well to note that the Gall Meridian Acupuncture Points 27 to 32 mark the general line of working: note, too, that Gall Meridian Points 28, 29 and 30 are key points of the thigh musculature.

When both sides have been done the Subject is again instructed to lie supine and to take one knee up towards the stomach, holding it there with his hands and extending the leg a little: the other foot remains resting on the

36

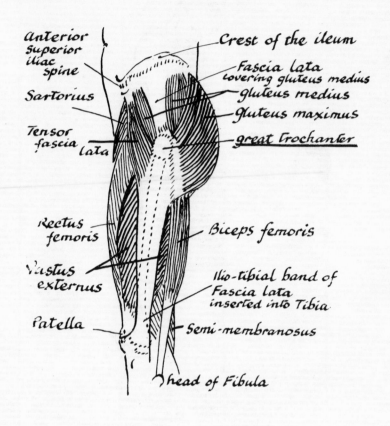

Anterior superior iliac spine

Crest of the ileum

Sartorius

Fascia lata covering gluteus medius

gluteus medius

Gluteus maximus

Tensor fascia lata

great trochanter

Rectus femoris

Biceps femoris

Vastus externus

Ilio-tibial band of Fascia lata inserted into Tibia

Patella

Semi-membranosus

head of Fibula

Diagram 19

table surface. The operator now gives a long, slow, deep and heavy stroke from the distal end of the biceps femoris along its medial edge as far as the origin; and a similar stroke lateral to the semitendinosus. This operation is known as 'freeing the hamstrings'. The operator uses his knuckles of one hand, guiding the strokes with the other hand. DO NOT TAKE ANY RISK OF SLIPPING, so guide the stroke. See diagram 20.

Both sides are then tested to ensure that they balance; that is to say, make sure they have both been freed, one as much as the other.

The Subject remains supine, taking up the first position of part 1, i.e. flexing the knees, dragging the heels.

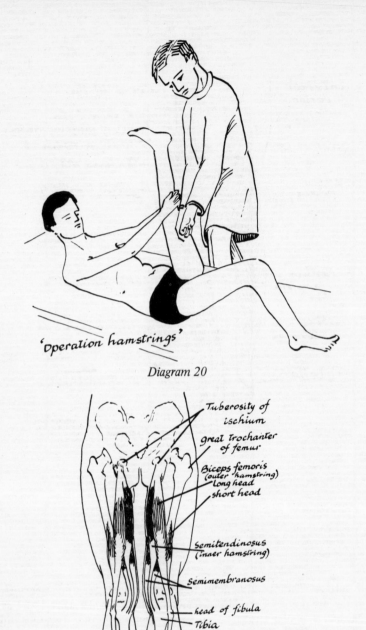

'Operation hamstrings'

Diagram 20

Tuberosity of
ischium

great trochanter
of femur

Biceps femoris
(outer hamstring)
long head
short head

Semitendinosus
(inner hamstring)

Semimembranosus

head of fibula

Tibia

Diagram 21

The Subject is instructed to raise the 'tip of his tail' taking his waist line (at the small of the back) into closer contact with the table (couch or floor) surface. What we want him to do is to lift the coccyx and sacrum in such a way 'that we can slide a hand, palm uppermost, under each buttock, to hook the last phalanges of middle and third finger over the sacrum and ileum, so that the sacrum and pelvis may be *pulled* away from the fifth lumbar vertebra. The Subject is asked to let his weight rest relaxed on the operator's fingers.

This operation, the 'sacrum pull', is done with the intention of imparting greater resilience to the sacro-lumbar 'disc'.

Diagram 22

Finally some attention is given to the neck. DO NOT FORGET TO WASH YOUR HANDS NOW, BEFORE DOING THE NECK.

Some work will be done on the neck area during every session until the seventh hour, when almost the whole session is devoted to the neck. At this first session we are not able to do more than lightly manipulate some outer muscle layers; but the basic manipulative movements follow the same pattern all the way through.

It will probably be noticed that in the supine position the chin is pointed too much up in the air, and the back of the head is not properly resting on the table surface. With a hand either side of the occiput the operator lifts the head and *eases* it, gently pulling and stretching the neck, towards the correct position, noting as he does so where tensions are trying to hold the head and neck. The finger ends of both hands work on the occipital attachment of the pars descendens of the trapezius (clavicular part), being careful not to press too heavily along the base of the skull.

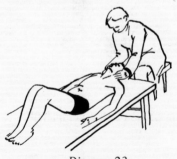

Diagram 23

The operator lifts and turns the Subject's head first to one side then to the other each time working a little on the upper attachments of the sterno-mastoid muscle.

39

In most subjects the whole of the neck area tends to be very much 'gummed up and thickened'; it will require *gradually* working into a flexible structure. Remember, it cannot be done all at once; and the whole of this area is sensitive. The illustrations should make it quite clear to the operator how to tackle these manipulations.

Acupuncture practitioners could usefully consult their charts as a reminder of the positioning of the following Acupuncture Points: Governor points 15 and 16, Bladder Meridian point 10, Gall Meridian points 12 and 20, Colon Meridian point 17, and Three-Heater Meridian points 16 and 17. These last two points are considered important, by the Chinese, for treating deafness, noises in the ears, eye congestions, oedema of the face, and inflammation of the parotids; and the two Governor points mentioned are important in treating congestive headaches, cerebral congestion, etc. While we are doing Progressive Vitality manipulations, however, the intention is NOT to treat any of the above mentioned conditions; *our intention is focussed on freeing the structures.* If we can do this the effect will be freer flow and interchange of all vital fluids, forces, energies, and so on, which, when free to do so will balance themselves naturally.

The Subject is now instructed to sit up, lean forward and rest his forehead on his knees, clasping his arms round his knees. The operator, with his knuckles, makes two strokes (one on either side of the spine) down the sacrospinalis from about the fifth thoracic vertebra to the sacrum. (This follows the Bladder Meridian from point 14 to point 26.)

Diagram 24

The First Treatment Session is now completed.

Session 2.

With the exception of a few minutes manipulating down the spine and on the neck musculature, the whole of this second treatment is spent on the structure between knee and ankle anteriorly, at the ankle joint, and on the foot.

The Subject is instructed to stand relaxed and upright. Watch the position in which he spontaneously places his feet. The average person stands with the heels only slightly apart and the feet pointing outwards forming an angle of 45° or more. Sometimes one foot is placed a little forward and sideways.

Toes pointing out is NOT the correct efficient stance: yet, in spite of this, we have met one 'posture specialist' who had foot outlines at the 45° angle painted on the floor where he asked his patients to stand to be photographed.

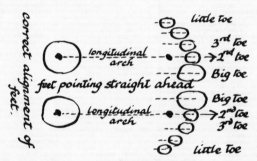

Diagram 25

In the relaxed standing position both feet should point straight ahead, the weight being borne on the anterior and posterior pillars of the longitudinal arch. At rest most of the sole of the foot is in contact with the ground; the arches become apparent as soon as muscle action begins.

The more a person's feet point outwards (like the hands of a clock at ten to two) the less likelihood is there of pliability in the feet. Turning the feet out is a way of walking with minimum flexion at the ankles and at the metatarsophalangeal articulations. When walking, the main propulsive force is (or should be) through the gastrocnemius and the 'hinge' joint at the ankle bringing pressure on the distal pillar of the longitudinal arch. The 'lever' action is at its most efficient when the feet point straight ahead.

During this treatment session our manipulations are aimed at helping the feet to assume correct alignment, by dispersing and freeing the various adhesions, immobilities, etc., which obstruct full and free pliability. To this end we must first assess the positioning of the major restrictions.

41

The Subject is now to be seated with his back supported upright, and with both legs extended. He is then instructed to dorsiflex and plantarflex his feet as far as he can and, at each position, to extend and flex his toes. The operator will thus get a good mental picture of the range and freedom of movement. He will begin to work on the less restricted limb.

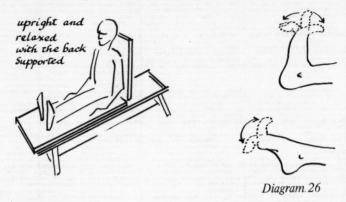

upright and relaxed with the back supported

Diagram. 26

DO NOT HURRY.

Remember that the whole foot is extremely sensitive, especially near the metatarso-phalangeal joints of big and second toe, deep in the plantar muscle layers. There is no need for the Subject to be given any pain: and it is very easy to cause considerable distress. There will be no pain if the operator takes his time and his intention is right.

The foot we have chosen to work on first is held with both hands in such a way that the thumbs can work on the axis through the malleoli. Start on the centre line of the dorsum of the foot and work from there towards each malleolus over the extensor tendon retinaculum. The tendons will also be worked between the thumb and forefinger, as shown in the drawing of typical manipulations. Just anterior to the malleolus the direction of the manipulative movement must be below the malleolus and posteriorly.

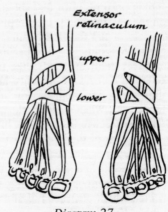

Extensor retinaculum
upper
lower

Diagram 27

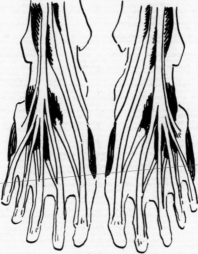

tendons of dorsi-flexors of the ankle
and the extensors of the toes

Diagram 28

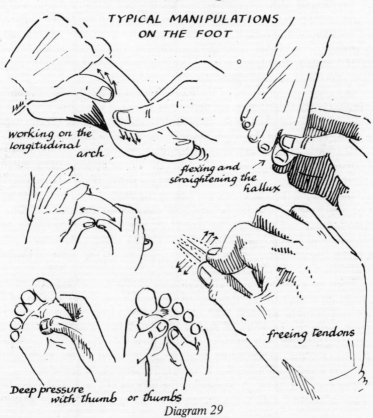

TYPICAL MANIPULATIONS
ON THE FOOT

working on the
longitudinal
arch

flexing and
straightening the
hallux

freeing tendons

Deep pressure
with thumb or thumbs

Diagram 29

43

As a reminder we note that anterior to the medial malleolus is the tibialis anticus muscle tendon; and posterior to the medial malleolus are the tendons of the tibialis posticus, the flexor digitorum longus, and the flexor hallucis longus. Behind the external malleolus are the tendons of the peroneus brevis and peroneus longus. Between the two malleoli, on the dorsum, are the tendons of the peronius tertius, extensor digitorum longus, extensor hallucis longus, and the tibialis anticus already mentioned.

All the extensor tendons should be palpated, worked, and freed as far as their insertions. The bodies of the following muscles should be thoroughly worked between first fingers and thumbs: extensor digitorum brevis, extensor hallucis brevis, abductor hallucis and abductor digiti quinti.

On the sole of the foot the plantar aponeurosis covers several layers of muscles and flexor tendons. The muscles of the first layer are: the Abductor hallucis, Flexor digitorum brevis and the Abductor digiti minimi; the muscles of the second layer are: the Flexor digitorum accessorius and the Lumbricales; the muscles of the third layer are: the Flexor hallucis brevis, Adductor hallucis, and the Flexor digiti minimi brevis. These three layers are shown in our drawings. The fourth layer, not shown, is made up of the interossei plantares which arise from the bases and medial sides of the shafts of the third, fourth and fifth metatarsals, and are inserted into the medial sides of the bases of the proximal phalanges of these same toes. The interossei dorsales will conveniently be worked at the same time; these muscles are bipennate, each arising by two heads from the adjacent sides of the metatarsals between which it is placed; their tendons insert into the bases of the proximal phalanges and into the dorsal digital expansions.

The principal functions of these muscles are to steady the toes and to help maintain the longitudinal and transverse arches of the foot.

Pay special attention to the third layer, aiming to add length and impart tone to the oblique and transverse heads of the adductor hallucis muscles.

If twenty minutes are allowed for work on the *sole* of each foot this will not be found too generous. One simply has to do as much as possible within the time. Allow five minutes per foot for the work on the malleoli and across the dorsum; include in this the freeing the head of the fibula. The work around the head of the fibula means thoroughly freeing and restoring to proper pliability and mobility the area of the insertion of the biceps femoris, the arcuate and lateral ligaments, and that part of the popliteus muscle that goes under the arcuate ligament. In this session we do not work on the knee joint as such.

When both lower limbs have been done as above, the Subject is instructed to sit on a chair (or on the edge of the working surface), and to let the head "hang forward and take the body slowly down towards the knees". The operator, with the knuckles of each hand in turn (the other supporting the shoulder so that the Subject does not fall forward) gives a long slow deep heavy stroke close to the spine from about the level of the angle of the scapula down as far as the lumbar vertebrae. This lengthens the back.

The operator, through supporting the subject at the shoulder, controls the movement. We are aiming here for a slow folding forwards as the knuckles

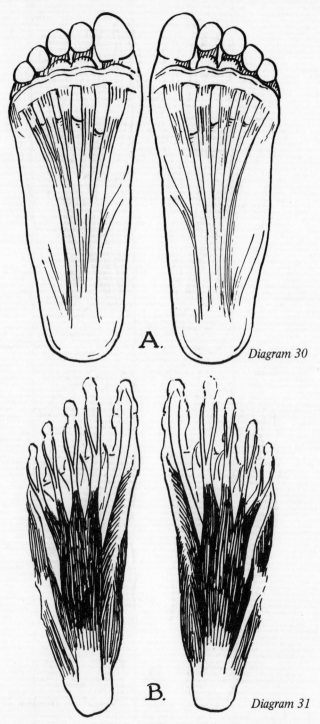

A.

Diagram 30

B.

Diagram 31

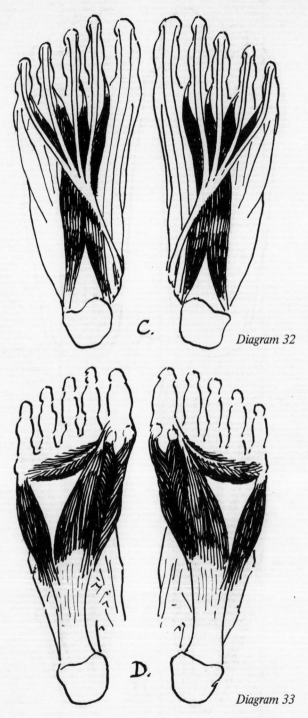

C.

Diagram 32

D.

Diagram 33

46

'peel the restrictions away downwards'. The illustration shows a (female) subject fully 'folded' at the end of the movement — but it is rarely ever achieved as fully as this.

Diagram 34

The Subject is instructed to get up slowly, resuming a standing position. He is told to try to visualise a string from the crown of his head pulling him up gracefully. This MUST be done slowly to avoid a possible momentary dizziness.

Whatever time is left is spent on further freeing the neck musculature as in the previous session.

The second session is now at an end.

Session 3.

At this session work is done on the shoulder girdle and on the pelvic girdle. The operator will need to assess each case as regards which girdle is to have priority, by deciding which girdle, in his opinion, is more restricted and 'tied-up'. In this instance the more restricted is to be tackled first. In the event of it being somewhat difficult to decide which girdle is to have priority of treatment it would be advisable to follow the general pattern of shoulder first in male subjects and pelvis in female subjects. Although this is a general rule it is a safe guide so long as the operator remembers that it is not *necessarily* so. If a wrong choice is made it simply means that more time is taken up because the operator will find that certain structures cannot be properly freed on account of their being held by others which should have been cleared before, and he therefore has to go back to work some areas over again. In any case when making a choice do not discount 'intuition'.

We assume, for the purpose of describing the manipulations, that our Subject is male and that the shoulder girdle is to be done first. The Subject is instructed to lie on one side. Place a small pillow under his head. The operator will sit behind him as in the illustration. When necessary one hand supports or holds the Subject's arm in a convenient position to enable the other hand to manipulate the tissues.

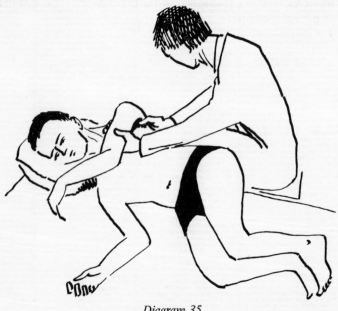

Diagram 35

48

Work begins on the flat tendon of the Teres major, which is inserted into the medial lip of the bicipital groove of the humerus, behind the tendon of the Latissimus dorsi. For a short distance along their lower borders these tendons are united. Close to the insertion of the Teres is part of the origin of the lateral and medial heads of the Triceps.

This grouping is worked between the thumb and fingers until the tissues are felt to be supple, free, and without adhesions. This manipulation will appear to give additional length to the Teres, thereby giving greater freedom and range to the scapula.

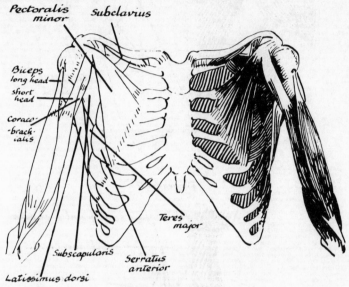

Diagram 36

Our drawing shows the interlacing of the Triceps, Latissimus dorsi, and Teres. Thumb and fingers will have to be pinched together quite forcefully (but carefully) to work *across* muscle fibres.

The fingers will be pressed firmly and deeply into all the muscles on the dorsum of the Scapula.

In order to follow out the rule, which we should never forget, 'periphery to core' the outer layers will receive first attention. That is to say the Deltoid will be grasped 'as a handful' and eased with a 'lifting away' movement. The Trapezius will be wrung with both hands along its upper part from the external occipital protruberance to the insertion of the superior fibres into the posterior border of the lateral third of the clavicle. The medial and inferior fibres will be given deep finger-working from the origins (ligamentum nuchae, spine of 7 C, and the spines of all the Thoracic vertebrae) to their insertions into the medial margin of the acromion and spine of scapula.

The upper border of the latissimus dorsi must be manipulated; and also the muscles above and below the spine of scapula (the supra-spinatus and

49

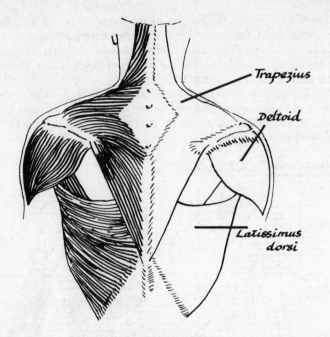

Diagram 37

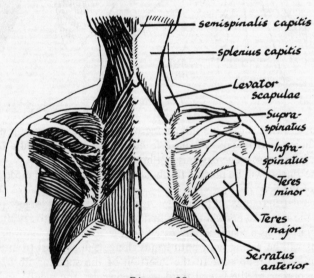

Diagram 38

infra-spinatus); work on the origin and insertion of the rhomboid, and on the insertion of the Levator scapulae. The origin of the Levator scapulae will now be more accessible when, at the end of this session, work is done on the neck musculature.

50

The operator will need to hold the Subject's arm in the raised position in order to reach and work on the Subscapularis, of which the anterior surface forms a considerable part of the posterior wall of the axilla.

It should now be possible for the operator to get a hand between the scapula and the thorax near the angle of scapula. For this manipulation the Subject is to be reminded to relax and allow the manipulation to happen. This movement must happen easily and must never be forced. It is accomplished by holding a hand flat on the thorax close to the angle and, with the other hand on the acromion moving the scapula up and down through its full range. The diagram should make this clear.

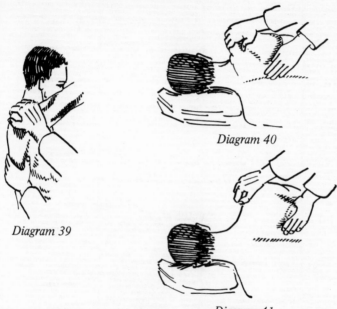

Diagram 40

Diagram 39

Diagram 41

The other half (or side) of the shoulder girdle is not to be touched until the pelvic girdle and the line joining the girdles on this first side have been done. The line which joins shoulder and pelvic girdles is an imaginary line drawn from the head of the humerus to the head of the femur.

Use fingers and thumbs of both hands to draw flesh *away* from this line. It is important that this line, linking the girdles, be established by the end of this third hour. Posterior to this line is the Latissimus dorsi, and anterior to this line are the digitations of the Serratus magnus and the Obliquus abdominis externus. If the shoulder girdle is done before the pelvic girdle (as our present example) start at the top of this line and work down towards the iliac crest: if the pelvic girdle is done first then work up the line towards the axilla.

The intention here is focussed on persuading any tissues that have 'wandered across the line' to resume their rightful position. Between the 10th rib and the iliac crest the operator will, with a spreading action (with his

51

thumbs), away from the axilla-femur line, separate the layers of the obliquus externus, obliquus internus, and the transversus abdominis. The rectus abdominis and pyramidalis are not touched at this session.

When the pelvis is reached the iliac crest is dealt with in a similar way to that in which the anterior border of the thoracic cage and diaphragm were 'peeled clean' so that bone contours are clearly felt.

The quadratus lumborum, though a relatively small muscle, is important on account of its attachments, i.e. the muscle arises from the ilio-lumbar ligament and iliac crest inserting into the medial half of the lower border of the 12th rib and, by four tendons, to the transverse processes of the upper four lumbar vertebrae. In proper tone the quadratus lumborum will pull the 12th rib down into position, fixing it, and steadying the origin of the diaphragm. Be careful with the 12th rib.

Work along the whole crest and inner lip of the iliac crest; manipulate as much of the origin of the iliacus muscle as can be reached. This large flat triangular muscle which fills the iliac fossa is, to us, one of the most important of all muscles, for it is directly connected to the key Core Structure. The insertion of the iliacus is into the lateral side of the tendon of the Psoas major, and some of its fibres are attached to the shaft of the femur below and in front of the lesser trochanter.

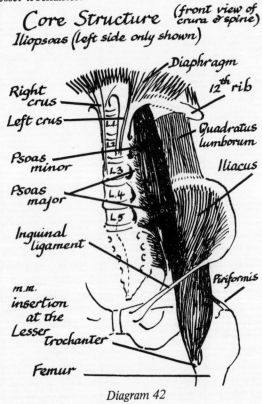

Core Structure (front view of crura & spine)
Iliopsoas (left side only shown)

Right crus
Left crus
Psoas minor
Psoas major
Inguinal ligament
m.m. insertion at the Lesser Trochanter
Femur

Diaphragm
12th rib
Quadratus lumborum
Iliacus
Piriformis

L.1
L.2
L.3
L.4
L.5

Diagram 42

52

The maintenance of the erect posture at the hip-joints *depends upon* perfect balance of tone between, on the one hand, the rectus femoris, psoas major and iliacus and, on the other hand, the extensors of the joints. Gray points out that it does not seem improbable that the Iliacus *functions mainly as a postural muscle.*[1]

Before doing the other side ask the Subject to get up and walk a few paces. He will probably (if your work has been well done) experience difficulty owing to a feeling of being unbalanced – one side feeling much longer than the other. The operator will have an opportunity of assessing how much has to be done to bring both sides to a state of balance.

When the other side is finished and both parties, i.e. Subject and Operator, are satisfied that the two sides are now well balanced, the Subject is instructed to sit with his knees drawn up, resting his forehead on them, and hands clasped round the knees. The operator, from behind the Subject, using the knuckles of both hands simultaneously, draws 'laterally-wandered' tissues towards the spine, mainly in the dorso-lumbar area. Again it must be stressed NOT to press too heavily on the 12th rib.

gathering the 'laterally-
-wandered' tissues

Diagram 43

The Subject is then instructed to lie supine, relaxed, and with knees flexed and feet resting on the working surface. Some work is now continued on the neck musculature. It will be noticed that it is now possible to get deeper into the neck muscles. Pay particular attention to the scaleni, splenius, and levator scapuli which are now more easily accessible; and attend to the trapezius upper fibres from the origin at the occipital bone and to the spine of the seventh cervical vertebra.

A few minutes work on the neck brings this third session to a close.

[1] Gray's Anatomy 31st edn. (1954) p.642. Longmans, Green & Co.

Session 4.

At this fourth treatment we shall be going deeper and deeper towards the core; our key structures for the session being the ischiae and pubes, and relationships *within* the pelvis. Therefore *when a male operator is working on a female subject it is advisable to have another woman present during this hour;* or, at the very least, arrange matters so that the door is not closed and people can be heard walking to and fro occasionally outside.

The Subject is instructed to lie down on one side, and a small pillow placed under his head. The operator sits behind the Subject, and places the Subject's upper leg forward with the knee supported by a firm cushion; he places the lower leg back and works on this lower leg.

Work will start on the foot at the insertion of the Achilles tendon, and very thoroughly deal with the area from the tendon to just anterior to the medial malleolus, below the malleolus, the whole area of the flexor retinaculum, following *up* the tendons of the tibialis posterior, flexor digitorum longus, and the flexor hallucis longus.

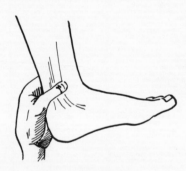

Diagram 44

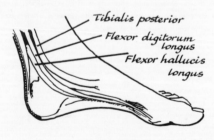

Diagram 45

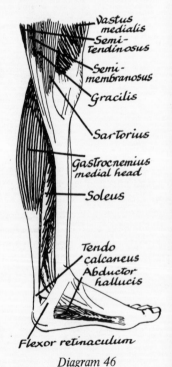

Diagram 46

54

Work up the leg behind the tibia with fingers or thumb going deeply into and separating the muscle structures of the tibialis posterior and flexor digitorum longus from those inserting into the Achilles tendon, namely, the soleus and gastrocnemius.

Make sure that the contours of the medial surface and medial border of the tibia are clean and clear. Follow the medial surface up to the insertions of the semitendinosus, gracilis, and the sartorius, and the insertion of the semi-membranosus on the medial condyle of the tibia.

A great deal of patient hard work must be done around the medial part of the knee joint to ensure freedom and flexibility of the tendon insertions. Gradually work up the medial aspect of the thigh. Both hands will be needed for the deep pressure and wringing manipulations on the vastus medialis, and deep pressure at the femoral attachments of the medial femoral muscles, i.e. gracilis, pectineus, adductor longus, adductor brevis and the adductor magnus.

DO NOT HURRY.

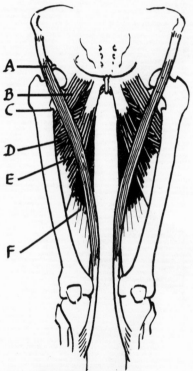

A   Sartorius m.
B   Pectineus m.
C   Lesser Trochanter
D   Adductor brevis m.
E   Adductor longus m.
F   Adductor magnus m.

Diagram 47

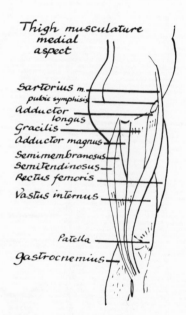

Thigh musculature medial aspect

Sartorius m.
pubic symphisis
Adductor longus
Gracilis
Adductor magnus
Semimembranosus
Semitendinosus
Rectus femoris
Vastus internus
Patella
gastrocnemius

Diagram 48

It may be necessary to try several times to reach the lesser trochanter to free the insertion of the psoas major tendon. Great care is needed when the operator is palpating the contours of, and working on, the pectineus and the adductors brevis, longus and magnus at their pubic attachments. The operator will need to adjust the position of the limb on which he is working in order that his extended first two digits may get in the small triangular gap to reach

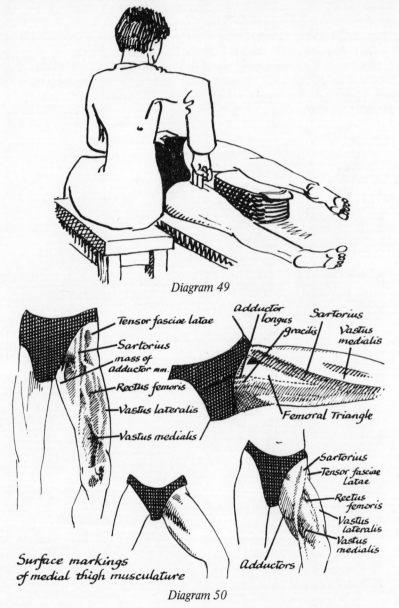

Diagram 49

Surface markings
of medial thigh musculature

Diagram 50

the lesser trochanter sufficiently to hook at least one finger tip round the psoas and iliacus tendon of insertion.

Intention coupled with visualization will here be the chief influential operative factor in freeing this structure.

DO NOT HURRY.

The operator must – let us re-emphasize, *must* – have a clear picture in his mind of the structures he is working on; there will then be no mistakes.

From this position the operator should be able to feel the contour of the inferior ramus of the pubis, the ramus of the ischium and the lateral portion of the inferior part of the tuberosity of the ischium. He should not only manipulate the adductor origins but reach well up through the pubes themselves.

The Subject is instructed to turn on to his other side, and this second side is treated as the first. When this has been done the Subject is instructed to lie supine and take his knees up to the abdomen, the hands holding the knees in position. The operator tests, by palpation, the position of the ischiae, and instructs the Subject to let one leg down, knee bent and relaxed, foot resting on the working surface. The knee must be kept toward the centre line and the limb not allowed to fall outwards.

The operator will now work along the hamstrings of the raised leg. He will need to stand leaning over the Subject so that he can put his full weight behind his extended arm, with his knuckles working along the hamstring distally to proximally (i.e. towards the ischial tuberosity, their origin).

This is similar to the way the hamstrings were worked during the first treatment session, but this time the operator is able to go deeper into the structures.

Repeat the process on the hamstrings of the other limb; and then instruct the Subject to take both knees up on to his abdomen again.

With fingers or thumbs work between the coccyx and the ischial tuberosity, on the sacro-tuberous ligament and the underlying muscles (the coccygeus, piriformis, obturator internus, levator ani and the transversus perinaei superficialis) and the ischial extremity of the ischio-cavernosus. It is important to striate the fibres of the coccygeus and *let it lengthen:* the finger tip can then be inserted under the end of the coccyx pulling it uncurled. Remember that throughout the whole treatment the operator never at any time enters *any* orifice.

It often happens that the coccyx, through some injury, curls inwards excessively. This should be uncurled *because* this will free the vital ganglion of impar.

The operator will have to use his discretion regarding how much work may suitably be done on this area – not all Subjects respond favorably. When this part has been done the area round the anus should *spread* and not be tensed, clenched, or drawn in.

The Subject is instructed to 'unbend', placing his feet once again on the working surface, knees flexed. The operator sits to one side and, working with both hands, frees the upper border of the pubes. The bone contours must be felt 'clean'.

The operator now gives the Subject a 'sacrum pull' as described in session 1.

The operator is then to wash his hands *before* working on the neck. Whatever time is left, if any, is now spent on the neck musculature. This has to be taken in small doses, that is why whenever time permits a little is done at the end of each session.

Session number four is now finished.

Session 5.

The third treatment session was largely focussed on freeing the shoulder girdle, while number four mobilized the pelvic girdle. It will now be noticed, however, that a residual immobility remains in the upper structures.

In this fifth treatment session one reaches these upper structures through the rectus abdominis. These anterior structures must now be dealt with because unless these are done one cannot get the rib cage properly freed and positioned. This freeing has to be done by releasing the crura and psoas major origins.

The Subject takes up the supine position (knees up, dragging the heels) as at the first treatment session.

The operator manipulates at the manubrio-sternal articulation using a technique closely akin to a conventional physiotherapy 'skin-rolling' massage, as well as firm spreading and pushing movements with the fingers. The whole length of the sternum is thus treated, further freeing the sterno-costal articulations and thoroughly cleaning the costal cartilages across the whole width of the rectus abdominis insertions into the cartilages of the fifth, sixth, and seventh ribs (the most lateral fibres inserting into the anterior extremity of the fifth rib, the most medial fibres are sometimes found connecting with the costo-xyphoid ligaments and the side of the xyphoid process itself).

'Skin-rolling'

Diagram 51

The rectus abdominis muscles are separated in the medial line by the linea alba, the medial origins interlace and connect with the ligamentous fibres covering the front of the pubis symphysis. The lateral borders of the muscles are marked by the linea semilunaris (9th costal cartilage to the pubic tubercle).

Not only are the *anterior* surfaces of the ribs and costal cartilages to be worked on, the fingers must also go well up under the ribs, and under the lateral borders of the rectus abdominis. Between the navel and pubes the fingers should be able to meet (almost) under the rectus.

GREAT CARE must be taken down the entire length of the rectus abdominis to work the fingers *away* from the centre line, down and up under the muscle, then medially. (see illustrations)

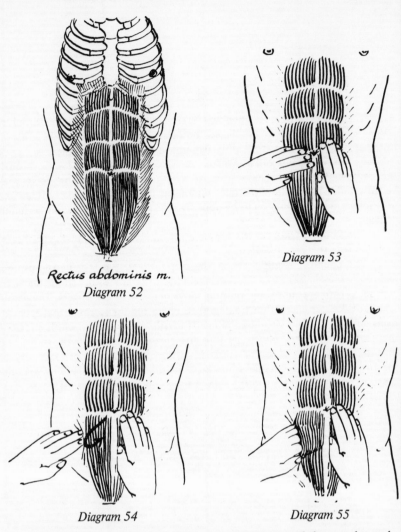

Rectus abdominis m.
Diagram 52

Diagram 53

Diagram 54

Diagram 55

At the pubis symphysis the rectus is very narrow and the muscle can be gripped between thumb and forefinger. The whole of the front of the abdomen must become a soft pliable and resilient structure; and the layers of the transversi and obliqui freed, giving *length* to the front of the body.

The anterior superior and inferior iliac crest is to be worked free, clean and clear.

The Subject is now to be encouraged to breathe quite gently, and to stay quiet and relaxed. Without relaxation the next manoeuvre will not be possible but, provided the Subject does remain relaxed, the seemingly impossible may now be attempted. It is not an easy manoeuvre to describe, and it must be taken quite slowly and sensitively. There must be no sudden movements to cause the Subject to tense the muscles.

The hand with extended fingers is held vertically with the finger ends close to the linea semilunaris. By very gradually increasing the pressure the fingers are allowed to sink slowly deep into the abdomen. The *intention* is to let the underlying internal organs and structures *move themselves easily and slowly out of the way to admit the fingers and their visualized extensions to reach and free the psoas attachment.*

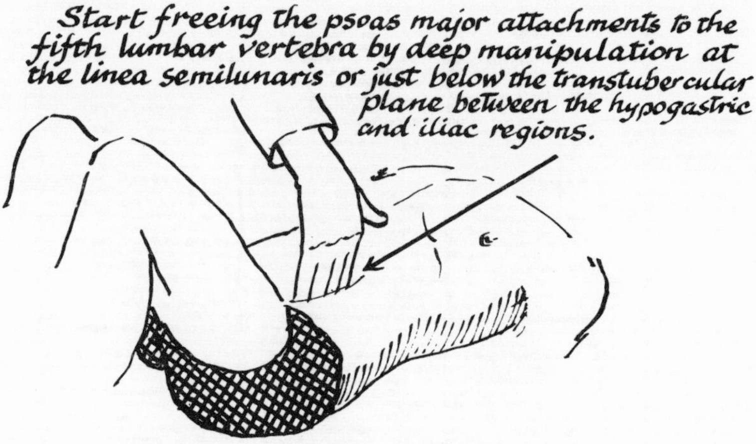

Start freeing the psoas major attachments to the fifth lumbar vertebra by deep manipulation at the linea semilunaris or just below the transtubercular plane between the hypogastric and iliac regions.

Diagram 56

DO NOT HURRY and, above all, do not force any organ or inner structure to make way — *the tissues will admit the fingers if they are given time to do so, and if the operator exerts very deep pressure gradually and sensitively.* There must be no sudden forcing. If a movement is too sudden the Subject will spontaneously tense the abdominal muscles and the operator's fingers will be thrown out.

Exactly how far the fingers do go in towards the anterior surfaces of the vertebrae we cannot say with any certainty; but, over and over again, during this manipulation we have had the Subject make some remark to the effect that "it feels as if you are touching the front of my spine".

When the hand is *slowly* lifted out — slowly to enable the tissues to ease their own way back into position — a remarkable change seems to have taken place: there seems now to be more length between rib-cage and pelvis, and the Subject experiences an abdominal freedom not felt before.

This operation is sometimes accompanied by release of emotional tensions, to which the operator should be tolerantly understanding. It is as if, now that the *physical* manifestation of built in repression and emotional tension has been removed there is no longer a physical 'prison' to hold the emotions; these are therefore released, and should be psychologically re-assessed so that there will not be any chance of a physical re-build.

It does sometimes happen that the operator does not seem to be able to get in sufficiently deeply to make the manipulation *felt* and, on this account, the release does not appear to be brought about. In such a case he

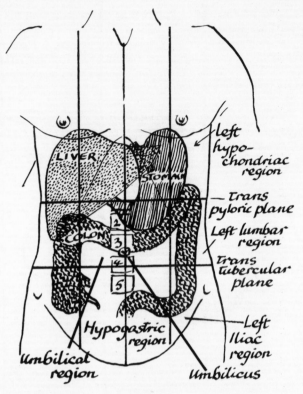

Diagram 57

must in no wise attempt to force it: and neither he nor the Subject are to feel discouraged nor despondant about it. If the *visualized intention* has been clear and concentrated, one must not assume that nothing has happened simply because there was no observable or tangible immediate result, *the change process will have been started,* but for some reason perhaps known only to the Subject's 'unconscious' may have to take place slowly with delayed action.

A little work on the neck brings this fifth session to a close. It should not be followed too closely by the next — there should be at least a forty-eight hour interval before the sixth treatment session begins.

Session 6.

This treatment session, and number seven which follows, has special importance from the acupuncture therapists' viewpoint. As we have already said, it is not *necessary* to know anything at all about Chinese Acupuncture to work the Progressive Vitality sequence and technique, and achieve first class results. We do, however, wish to make it clear to both acupuncteurs and physiotherapists that the knowledge of one system adds to appreciation of the other, thus being to some degree complementary.

The particular significance of the two areas (lower limb, knees to toes, and upper limb, elbows to finger-tips) being that within them are placed the Chinese acupuncture Five Elements Points. The Five Elements therapy method is not only an advanced method but it is also a *simple* method of quite remarkable efficacy. Some acupuncture practitioners use only the Five Elements method.

A powerful link between Progressive Vitality manipulative treatment and Chinese acupuncture treatment is this: Exact and detailed knowledge of anatomical structures enables the location of the Chinese points to be found with far greater precision and, similarly, an accurate knowledge of acupuncture point placing indicates areas where maximum flexibility and mobility is vital to health and economy.

It is a *general* guide to locating acupuncture points that at the acupuncture point a slight (sometimes almost imperceptible) depression or hollow can be felt. An anatomist realises that these hollows or depressions are of the kind that occur at and are formed by crossings, meeting or interlacing of tendons and ligaments, and at attachments of muscles, ligamants and so on to bone, etc., etc. In other words: *There is an anatomical structural reason for every palpable detail* such as these slight depressions at acupuncture points.

The Subject is instructed to sit (as at the beginning of Session 2) with the back supported and the legs straight out in front.

The transverse arch of each foot in turn is worked to a pliable structure at the metatarsophalangeal articulations. Both hands will be needed and with strong firm grip give many rapid flexing and double-flexing movements. The longitudinal arch will also be freed by dorsi-flexing the foot between fingers and thumbs. The Subject is reminded to relax the foot and allow this flexing to be done.

Both feet are to be done before instructing the Subject to lie prone.

All the calf muscles must now be kneaded, wrung, and generally manipulated into pliability. Considerable pressure may be required, and this must be taken slowly, otherwise it can be very painful. As we have said throughout: There is no need to cause pain. If pressure is applied gradually, with the intention of turning gel into sol to the point of 'ungumming' adhesions, the tissues will respond.

Prone : with feet supported or overhanging

Diagram 58

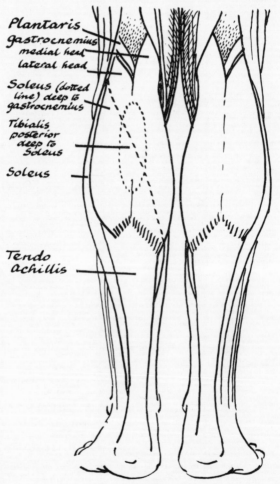

Plantaris

gastrocnemius
   medial head
   lateral head

Soleus (dotted
line) deep to
gastrocnemius

Tibialis
posterior
deep to
Soleus

Soleus

Tendo
Achillis

Diagram 59

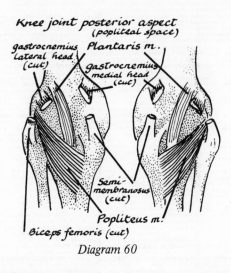

Knee joint posterior aspect
(popliteal space)

gastrocnemius
lateral head
(cut)

Plantaris m.

gastrocnemius
medial head
(cut)

Semi-
membranosus
(cut)

Popliteus m.

Biceps femoris (cut)

Diagram 60

Thumbs and fingers have much work to do in the popliteal area where the two heads of the gastrocnemius attach and run close to the insertions of the semi-membranosus and semi-tendinosus medially and the tendons of the biceps femoris (long and short heads) laterally. All the muscles at the back of the thigh will require thorough wringing, kneading, and deep pressure.

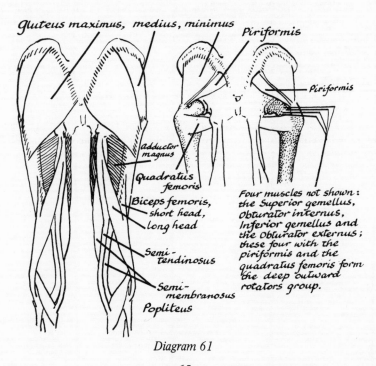

Gluteus maximus, medius, minimus

Piriformis

Piriformis

Adductor
magnus

Quadratus
femoris

Biceps femoris,
short head,
long head

Semi-
tendinosus

Semi-
membranosus

Popliteus

Four muscles not shown:
the Superior gemellus,
Obturator internus,
Inferior gemellus and
the Obturator externus;
these four with the
piriformis and the
quadratus femoris form
the deep outward
rotators group.

Diagram 61

65

Towards the origins of the hamstrings the manipulation will be deep, heavy, in the direction towards the ischial tuberosity underneath the gluteus maximus, i.e. up under the transverse buttock fold.

Striate the gluteal fibres with heavy pressure movements across the direction of the fibres. This may need to be done with the operator's full weight.

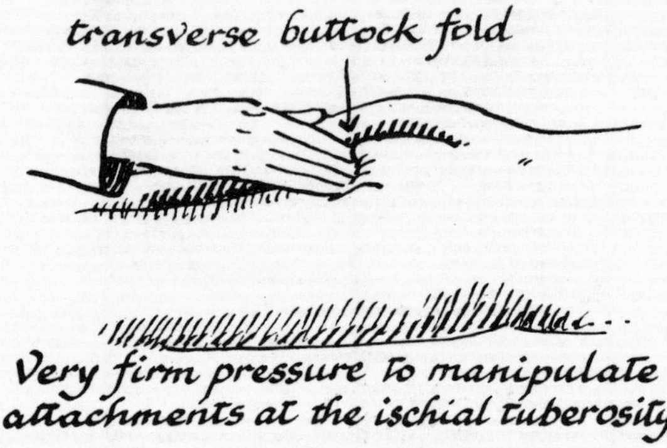

transverse buttock fold

Very firm pressure to manipulate attachments at the ischial tuberosity

Diagram 62

When the buttock muscles are freed the underlying bone contours should be clearly palpable.

Complete one limb and then ask the Subject to stand up and walk about a few steps. The difference in length between the two limbs should be so marked that the Subject tends to 'stagger'. This is a sign that the 'freeing process' has been effective.

With the Subject supine, knees flexed, give a 'sacral pull' as described in session One.

THE OPERATOR WILL NOW WASH HIS HANDS before working on the Subject's neck.

If a little work has been done on the neck at the end of each session so far, by the end of this sixth session the outer layers of the neck musculature should have been freed. The next session, number seven, deals with the deep muscles of the neck.

Session 7.

During this seventh session we go deeply into the structures which form the 'weaving' between the shoulder girdle and core (diaphragm), and between head and shoulder girdle. We also deal with the too often wholly neglected muscle structures — those of the face.

The Subject is instructed to lie supine, knees flexed, and to be as thoroughly relaxed as he is able. At this point in the Progressive Vitality treatment quite a high degree of relaxation should be possible.

The general flexibility and relaxation of the neck must be tested and assessed. Throughout this session's work on the neck there will need to be frequent tests, and alternating work — first on one side then on the other. The Subject will *need* the frequent head turnings, testing movements, rolling from side to side, and so on, in order that he shall not tire. The operator will gradually go deeper and deeper, but must be content to do so a little at a time (ever so many times of course).

It needs to be impressed on the Subject that, unless he is specifically asked to make a movement, he is to remain fully relaxed and let the operator do all the moving.

The principal testing movements are:

i. Head rolling from side to side. How easily does it roll and how far?

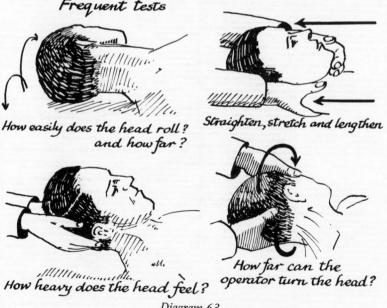

Frequent tests

How easily does the head roll? and how far?

Straighten, stretch and lengthen

How heavy does the head feel?

How far can the operator turn the head?

Diagram 63

67

ii. Lengthening, straightening or stretching the back of the neck. How easily and how far?

iii. Feeling the weight of the head. It should feel heavy.

iv. How far and how easily can the operator turn the Subject's head to left or right?

The operator will need to keep alert to notice where restrictions still remain, easing always a little at a time.

Although so much work will already have been done on the sterno-cleido-mastoidus, we follow our principle 'periphery to core' and therefore even in this session begin work on this muscle.

Turn the Subject's head to one side: not just rolling it to one side, but turn it by lifting the back of the head with one hand under the head, and the other hand holding the Subject's forehead. For example: If we wish to turn the head to his left, lift his head with the right hand; turn his head, let it rest on the surface and hold it firmly in the turned position with the left hand. The knuckles of the right hand are now used to draw the sterno-cleido-mastoidus (near its occipital attachment) towards the back of the neck. The knuckles should come some distance back and along the occiput. This will enable the Subject to carry his head more centrally and not too far forward. The majority of people carry the head too far forward.

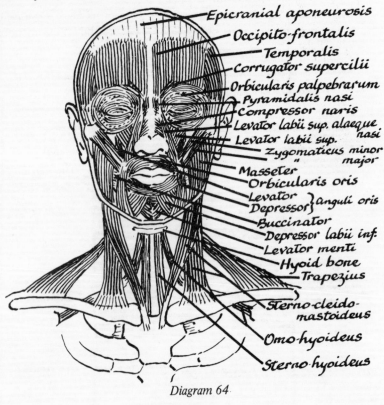

Diagram 64

The sterno-cleido-mastoidus usually gives a lot of trouble, being more or less seriously 'glued up' with adjacent structures, thereby giving corresponding trouble with the clavicle, first rib, and sternum.

Release the clavicular attachment, work thoroughly round the manubrium and the first rib where it can be reached.

The trapezius muscle, occipital attachment, must also be heavily persuaded towards the back.

Deep to the sterno-cleido-mastoidus is the levator scapulae which originates on the transverse processes of the four upper cervical vertebrae, inserting into the vertebral border of the scapula. Shortening, tension and immobility in the levator scapulae are often linked with psychological problems of 'built-in fear', or with 'carrying heavy burdens'.

The finger-tips should be able to curl under the rim of the occiput.

While the head is turned to the left and held in this position by the operator's left hand, reach with the right hand underneath to the other side to manipulate the splenius capitis and the scaleni (anterior, medius, and posterior).

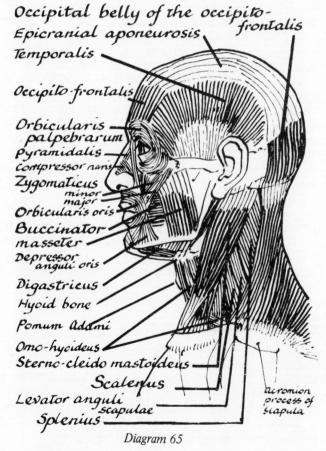

Diagram 65

69

Remember to keep turning the Subject's head; work alternating sides, going deeper each time.

DO NOT HURRY AND DO NOT USE FORCE. The tissues must be 'melted', 'softened', and 'persuaded'; even if at times quite heavily.

The thumbs and finger-tips will work on the external surface of the mandible, thoroughly freeing and striating the fibres of the masseter, platysma, and the buccinator, depressor anguli oris, depressor labii inferioris and the mentalis: cleaning the bone contours and working under to the lower part of the medial surface, reaching up as far as possible towards the origin of the mylohyoid, insertion of the medial pterygoid and anterior belly of the digastric muscle.

The whole of the area and structures around, above and below the hyoid bone will need *very sensitive and careful* working with finger tips. The area is not painful in the same sharp way the feet are painful, but pressure and manipulation can cause considerable discomfort and distress. It will generally be found that many emotional problems are built-in under the mandible.

The operator's intention must be to free to full flexibility and mobility *all* the muscles either arising from or inserting into the hyoid (supra- and infra-hyoid groups). The supra-hyoid muscles are: The digastricus, stylohyoideus, mylohyoideus, and geniohyoideus; and the infra-hyoid muscles are: The sternohyoideus, sternothyroideus, thyreohyoideus, and the omohyoideus.

In addition to the muscles of mastication (masseter deep and superficial heads, temporalis and the pterygoideus lateralis amd medialis) all the muscles of facial expression must be freed. Included in these muscles of facial expression will be the muscles of the scalp, the frontal and occipital bellies of the occipitafrontalis. The frontal belly is associated with expressions of surprise and terror.

The three muscles of the eyelids are: Levator palpebrae superioris, orbicularis oculi (which in old age forms the crow's feet), and the corrugator, the frowning muscle or the 'suffering indicator' muscle.

The four muscles of the nose, being small may not be easily separately palpable but should not be overlooked. These are the procerus (which makes the transverse wrinkles over the bridge of the nose), compressor naris, depressor septi, and the dilator naris.

Merely because a muscle is small is no justification for concluding that only a small amount of energy can be 'locked up' there. An apparently disproportionate amount of 'psychological energy' can be 'tied up' in the face muscles.

The muscles of the mouth are:

(a) Levator labii superioris alaeque nasi, the muscles which express contempt and disdain.

(b) Levator labii superioris, the 'sadness' muscle which assists in forming the naso-labial furrow.

(c) Zygomaticus minor which assists the formation of the naso-labial furrow.

(d) Zygomaticus major, the laughing muscle.

(e) Levator anguli oris.

(f) Mentalis, often associated with expression of doubt and disbelief.

(g) Depressor labii inferioris, sometimes called the 'irony' or 'simulated ignorance' muscle.

(h) Depressor anguli oris.

(i) Buccinator, the 'trumpet blower'.

(j) Orbicularis oris, which is not a simple sphincter but is partly composed of fibres from the other muscles.

(k) The Risorius which produces a somewhat unpleasant grin.

The 'thousand-and-one' subtleties and shades of expression result from combinations of movement of the above muscles, we have given only the simplest of hints concerning expression.

When the neck, head, and face muscles have been thoroughly done as described above, the Subject is told to sit upright on a chair. The operator stands behind him and places the closed fists, one on either shoulder, as close to the neck as possible, and, pressing *very heavily* on the trapezius, draws the flesh back and towards the median line, telling the Subject at the same time to 'take the top of his head up towards the ceiling'.

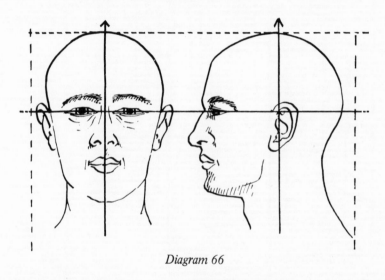

Diagram 66

The 'top of the head' point is shown on the diagram. About 1½ inches posterior to this top point, on the median line, is a highly important Chinese Acupuncture point (Pae Roe) known as a point 'for all that falls'. Scalp immobility at this point is often found in people suffering with any kind of prolapse (including haemorrhoids).

Attention must now be given to the upper limb, from the tips of the fingers to the head of the humerus; and all muscles up to and including the biceps, coracobrachialis, triceps, and the humeral attachments of the subscapularis, teres minor and major, and the latissimus dorsi.

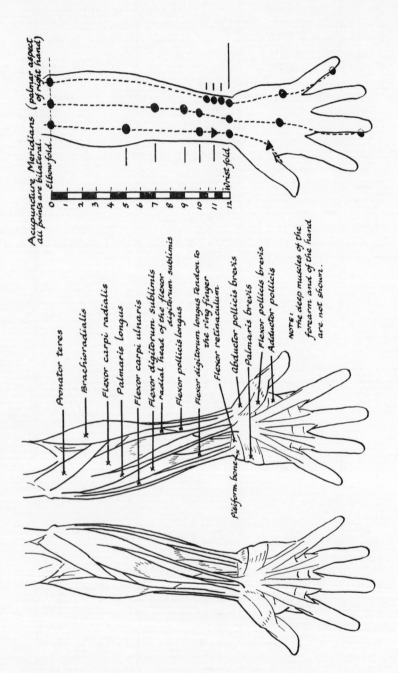

Acupuncture Meridians (palmar aspect of right hand)
all points are bilateral.

Elbow fold.

Wrist fold.

0 1 2 3 4 5 6 7 8 9 10 11 12

Pronator teres
Brachioradialis
Flexor carpi radialis
Palmaris longus
Flexor carpi ulnaris
Flexor digitorum sublimis radial head of the flexor digitorum sublimis
Flexor pollicis longus
Flexor digitorum longus tendon to the ring finger
Flexor retinaculum
Abductor pollicis brevis
Palmaris brevis
Flexor pollicis brevis
Adductor pollicis
Pisiform bone

NOTE: the deep muscles of the forearm and of the hand are not shown.

Diagram 67

72

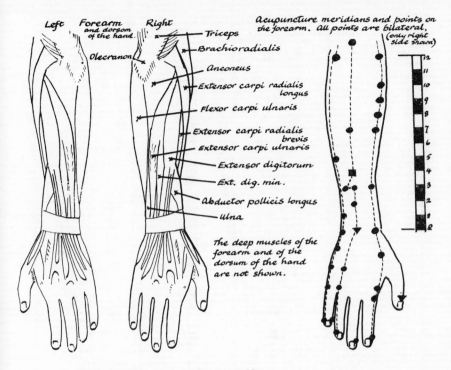

Left Forearm Right
   and dorsum
   of the hand.

Olecranon

Acupuncture meridians and points on
the forearm. All points are bilateral,
(only right
side shown)

Triceps

Brachioradialis

Anconeus

Extensor carpi radialis
        longus

Flexor carpi ulnaris

Extensor carpi radialis
        brevis

Extensor carpi ulnaris

Extensor digitorum

Ext. dig. min.

Abductor pollicis longus

Ulna

The deep muscles of the
forearm and of the
dorsum of the hand
are not shown.

Diagram 68

This seventh session, on account of the work done on the FACE, and on the upper limb BELOW THE ELBOW; and the sixth session on account of work done on the lower limb BELOW THE KNEE, have special importance for acupuncture therapists. ALL the Chinese FIVE ELEMENTS points are located on the upper and lower limbs; and ALL the twelve Organ Meridians have a first or a last point on hands or feet (3 first & 3 last on fingers, 3 first & 3 last on toes), on the face there are 3 first and three last points, the remaining 3 first and 3 last are on the thorax. Also on the face are the last points of the Conception and Governor Meridians. Both these are median line meridians, one anterior and one posterior, their first points being at the centre of the perineum and the tip of the coccyx respectively.

The seventh session has now been completed, and the operator is faced with making a decision whether to include two short additional sessions 7b & 7c, or next time to go straight into the eighth session.

The reason for this possibility is that by the end of the seventh session the loosening and freeing has not yet reached sufficiently deeply, one or other of the girdles may still appear too restricted. This will not ordinarily be the case if the work has been slow, thorough and competent; even then if the extra sessions have to be done the eventuality is not necessarily a reflection on the way the previous have been done. Some cases will present problems, deep-seated problems, that could not have appeared earlier.

73

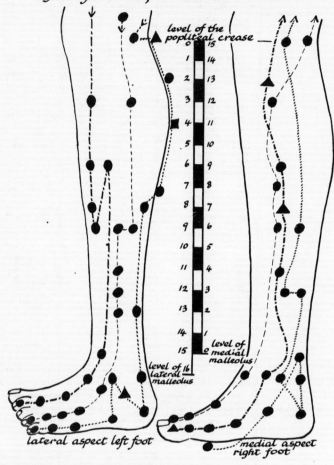

Acupuncture meridians and points on the leg and foot. All points are bilateral.

Diagram 69

The operator asks the Subject to walk about, move his limbs, and say how it all feels to him. The operator will use his eyes, hands, ears, and judgement to assess whether, in the case now infront of him, there is an immobility in the pelvic or shoulder girdle so restricting the other girdle that the core is hindered from 'organizing itself'. If there is any restriction arrange for the two short (or together in one longer) sessions, before going on to the eighth.

74

Sessions 7b & 7c.

In four Subjects out of five, whether male or female it will be the pelvic girdle which will need attention first. If the pelvic girdle, or lower half does in fact need attention work on any of the following areas. If necessary work on all of them.

Pelvic girdle,
Feet, knees, Rectus femoris,
Anterior iliac crest,
Ischial tuberosity,
Ramus,
Sacrum,
Hamstrings,
Acetabulum,
12th rib.

After having checked all the above and done what appears needed, give a 'Sacrum pull'. This should not be omitted. Then, with the Subject in the sitting position deal with the dorsal-lumber area and finish with the 'pressure on the shoulders at the sides of the neck, top point of the head reaching up towards the ceiling'. Half an hour, at this stage, should be ample to enable both sides to be done.

This is then followed by 7c, the shoulder girdle or thorax.

With the Subject on his side, check over very thoroughly, and do whatever freeing appears needed in these areas:

Rib cage, drawing the flesh away from the axiliary line towards the spine,
Base of scapula,
Iliac crest,
Quadratus lumborum,
Trapezius,
All round the humerus and acromion process,
Into the Teres (from back and front),
Pectoralis,
Clavicle,
Levator scapulae.

If earlier work on the neck has been regular and thorough there will probably be only a few deep adjustments to be made to the neck musculature. Finish this Session also with the 'top point of the head' manipulation.

In our own experience we have found it advisable to allow a full week's interval before attempting the final (Eighth) Session. This is to allow time for the 'self-adjustment' or 'self-organizing' to take place — it *can* now take place.

75

Session 8.

Up to this point of the treatment, during the first seven sessions, we have focussed our attention on parts, areas, limbs, groupings, and so on, seeing our Subject in terms of Shoulder girdle + Thorax + Abdomen + Pelvic Girdle.

This we have had to do because we were faced, from the first session, with a randomness rather than an ordered pattern. All the parts, it is true, belonged to one human being, but there did not appear to be a co-ordinated integrity. When this one human being walked from one side of the room to the other it is true that all of him went but, owing to various immobilities, restrictions and tensions, there was not an harmonious flow of movement.

We tackled area by area and, having dispersed immobilities, we related the areas to one another from periphery to core: so we should by now have in front of us an integrated organism. But we want more than an organism functioning efficiently and economically within its own boundaries (inside its own skin): we want to see this economy extended to an efficient relatedness to the environment.

It will be appreciated that our orientation is fundamentally different from that of the first seven treatments. This time we are concerned with the inter-relatedness of the whole organism and the earth's field. This is likely to be a long session, and 1¼ (one and a quarter) hours should be allowed.

We ask the Subject to walk about, sit down, stand up, take hold of something and put it down again, and so on. We watch him move. We watch the joints (hinges) in action.

The actual manipulative movements when we work on tendons, muscles, fascia, ligaments, etc., will be similar to those to which the operator has already become accustomed, but the *intention* will principally be to ease the limbs or parts into their proper *functional* position. Probably the greater part of this session's work will be made up of a number of quite minor adjustments and balancings. It is not possible to lay down a more or less rigid mechanical routine to be followed; because for each client this last hour will tend to be quite individual − it will all depend upon what has come to the surface since the previous session, and what refinements of balancings are needed.

We can, however, give a guide list of what is to be checked, and make a note or two about each item's features or characteristics: what the movement should be like, and what should be the quiet relaxed appearance.

We must bear in mind that our present task is to establish the 'right-angled relatedness'. The three directions, each at right angles to the other two, are: *Vertical,* Up & Down; *Lateral,* Side to Side; *Sagittal,* Forwards & Backwards.

76

For convenience we can group the items as follows:

i.   (a) Feet, (b) Knees, (c) Hips.

As we have already said in the early part of this book, the correct position for the feet is pointing straight ahead. The weight bearing parts of the foot being the heel pad and the pad at the base of the big and second toes. The ankle joint, or hinge between leg and foot, has its axis passing laterally at the level of the malleoli, parallel to the ground and at right angles to the sagittal plane. The movement from full dorsi-flexion to full plantar-flexion should be a smooth and steady movement in this sagittal plane without sudden movements or erratic deviations.

The knee joint should also have its axis parallel to the ground and at right angles to the sagittal plane. The knees should point forwards; not outwards nor inwards but forwards. Check that this is so, and that there is smooth movement from extension at the knee joint to full flexion and back again to extension.

The hip joint, which is not ginglymous, has a much wider range of movement, but nevertheless it should be able to allow the thigh to move in the sagittal plane as, for example, when walking the knee should move straight ahead. This means that there will be some rotation at the hip joint.

The action of walking is not a series of acts of putting one *foot* forward after the other. The focus is not on moving the foot, but on moving the *thigh,* taking one *knee* forward after the other. Leg and foot movements are simply adjustments. The work is done by hip and thigh musculature, not by leg and foot muscles, which are steadiers and balancers.

ii.   (d) Spinal joints.

There is only a small amount of movement possible at each spinal articulation. The total allows a smooth bending forwards or sideways or arching backwards, and a rotation between pelvic and shoulder girdles. It is important that every one of the joints be checked and freed (if not already free). The small of the back, or back of the waist-line, is generally carried too far forward, so that the buttocks 'stick out behind'.

Try to get the sacro-lumbar joint and the lumbar joints flexible and so eased that the pelvis tilts more towards the back; that is to say 'with the tail turned more under'.

When the Sacrum Pull is made it should be experienced as if each lumbar vertebra were a link in a chain able to move individually and brought into contact with the working surface one after the other (from the first to fifth and finally the sacrum itself).

iii.   (e) Wrist, (f) Elbow, (g) Shoulder.

In a relaxed standing position or when walking the backs of the hands should face forwards *not* sideways. The elbow should point slightly outwards. When the arm is lifted sideways the forearm should hang loosely down with the back of the hand forwards. The range of movement at the shoulder joint is very great indeed. Some authorities attribute this characteristic to the brachiating habits of our pre-human tree-living ancestors.

When reaching out to grasp something the general principle is similar to that governing knees and feet; that is to say: Do not focus attention on moving the *hand* towards the object; move the upper part first, taking the elbow out a little, swinging the arm forwards (between the pectoralis and latissimus dorsi) so that the *elbow* moves in the direction of the object and, at the appropriate distance away, let the forearm muscles and hand muscles make the final adjustments. Not only will such movements be more graceful, they will also be more economical, i.e. less effort will be needed because the responsibility for the movement will be on the large muscles well able to make the movement with little effort.

iv.   (h) neck, (i) cervico-occipital junction.

The head should balance on a relaxed neck, so that in the normal standing position the eyes look to the distant horizon, i.e. in a horizontal parallel to the earth's surface. The straight ahead or sagittal direction being from the mid-line of the nose to the centre line of the back of the head.

The 'top-point' of the head is important not only at this stage and during this session, but will be so from now onwards for the remainder of the Subject's lifetime.

The Subject is told to try to visualize an invisible thread going upwards from this 'top-point' by which he is suspended from heaven in contact with earth. Man lives at the junction plane of Heaven and Earth: the directive, purpose and power should be acknowledged as coming from on high.

When rising from a sitting position the focus of attention is on being *lifted from this top-point,* not on pushing oneself up by one's own muscular effort. When walking up a flight of steps it is easier if the focus of attention is on being lifted by the invisible thread, rather than on pushing the body weight upwards through the effort made by the muscles between the pelvis and the soles of the feet.

The Subject is instructed to sit upright on a chair, the operator, standing at one side, lifts him off the chair or eases his weight off the chair by holding one hand at the base of the occiput and the other hand under the Subject's chin. The spine should be felt to dangle and ripple rather like a chain (or child's string of conkers).

If photographic records are being kept, take the After Eight picture. The difference between the Before and After pictures is usually quite startling. The photograph illustrations are typical of results we ourselves have achieved. Any conscientious practitioner should be able to do as well; he may get even better results.

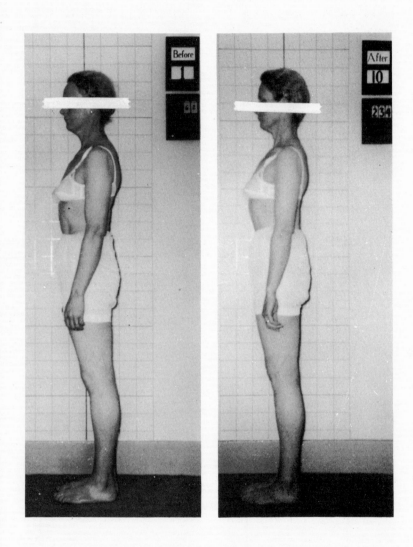

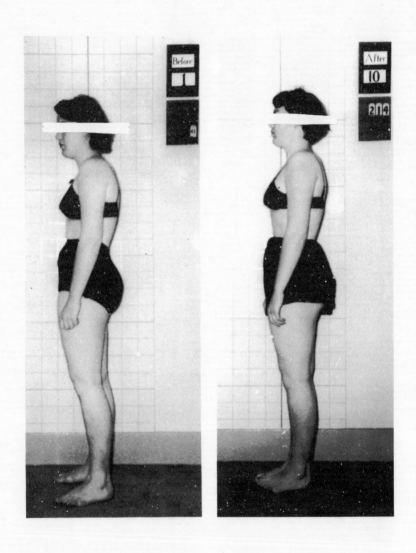

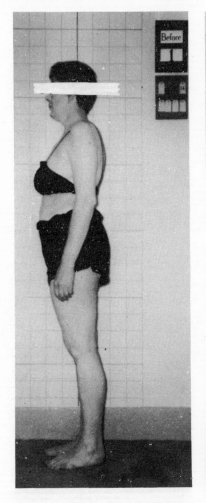 

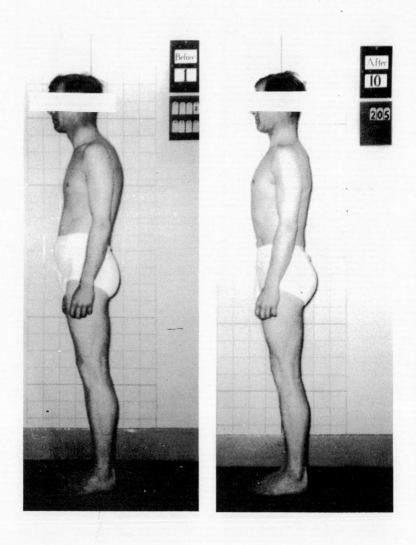